MADISON SQ
GARDEN
RINGLING BROS
BARNUM AND BAILEY
CIRCUS
TWICE DAILY - INCL. SUN.
TICKETS NOW ON SALE
AT BOX OFFICE
Advance Sale of Circus Tickets
Liggett's Drug Store
PRESCRIPTIONS
SODA · DRUGS
HATTER
DRUGS

GARDEN *of* DREAMS

STEWART, TABORI & CHANG | NEW YORK

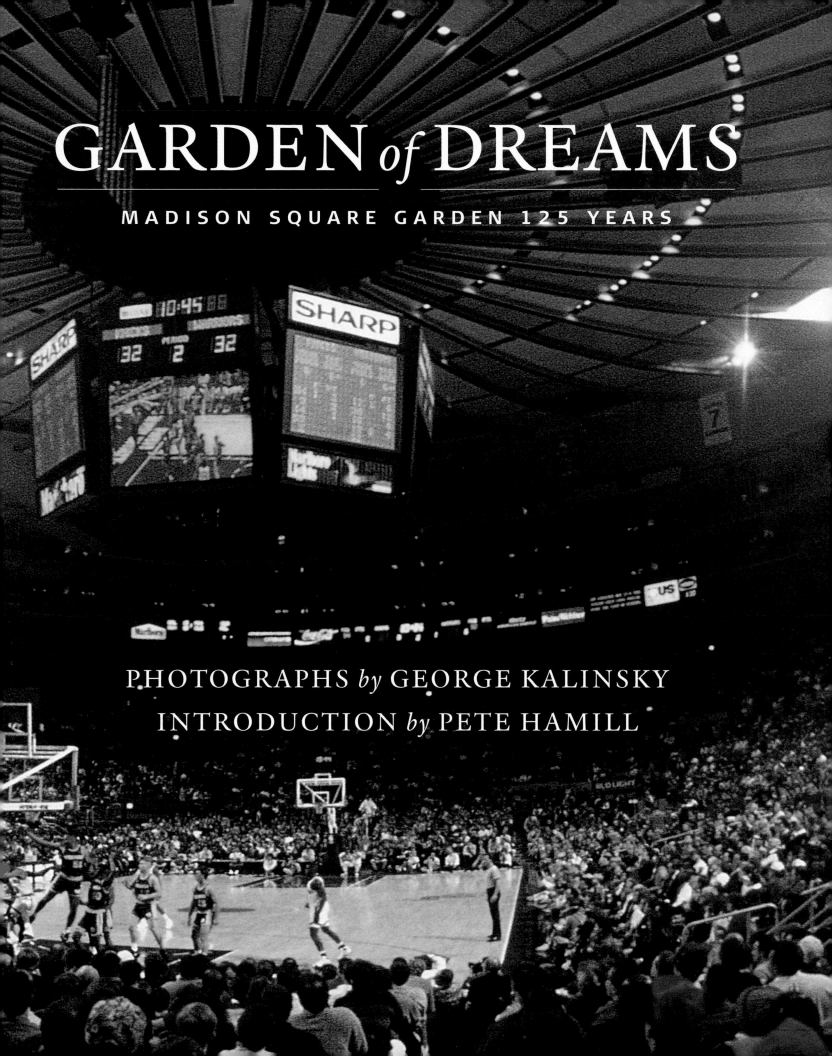

GARDEN *of* DREAMS

MADISON SQUARE GARDEN 125 YEARS

PHOTOGRAPHS *by* GEORGE KALINSKY

INTRODUCTION *by* PETE HAMILL

To the Memory of Marc Lustgarten

Acknowledgments

This book is a tribute to the many great performers who have graced the Garden with athletic
and artistic excellence, and to the many skilled, enthusiastic, and creative associates
with whom I have had the privilege of working.

The creation of this book was a team effort, and I would like to thank the following people:
all the marvelous celebrities who gave graciously of their valuable time to tell their Garden stories;
Pete Hamill, who enthusiastically wrote the superb introduction; Leslie Stoker, our publisher, whose vision
and determination made this book a reality; Rebecca Taylor, who spent endless hours
managing this project, providing her expertise to every creative and editorial aspect of the book;
Anne Marie Dunleavy, for her great efforts with our celebrity contributors; Cara Taback, who was always
there to provide invaluable research, editorial assistance, and suggestions; Sarah Miller, who kept
the daily operations of the MSG Photo Department flowing during the compilation of this book;
Galen Smith, STC art director, and designer Geoff Ledet, for the beautiful design; STC editor Jennifer Eiss
for helping pull it all together; Gary Stern for his contribution to the text, and Dennis D'Agostino
for providing the captions; Jennifer Unter, for her support; and my wife, June, my angel and best friend,
who always brings inspiration and joy, and our family, who have all enjoyed the magic of the Garden.

Madison Square Garden is committed to two special charities:
The Madison Square Garden Cheering for Children Foundation and
The Lustgarten Foundation for Pancreatic Cancer Research.

May 2004

Dear Friends:

New York City has long been known as the cultural capital of the world, and there is no better way to demonstrate that claim than by looking at the history of Madison Square Garden. From the "Fight of the Century," to John Lennon's last appearance, the Garden has seen some of the most historic performances in sports and entertainment. For 125 years, New Yorkers have built generations of memories by attending hockey and basketball games, the circus, and concerts given by some of the world's most legendary entertainers.

In 1879, the Garden was built in Madison Square because the community needed a place to congregate for conferences, see sports competitions, and present entertainment. Four buildings and more than a century later, the Garden is still the center of New York City's entertainment, and continues to reflect the vision of Stanford White and Tex Rickard. Whether it's a sold-out concert, or a Rangers or Knicks game, New Yorkers have been collecting first-hand accounts of some of the most memorable moments in history – and all because of the Garden.

Madison Square Garden represents not only the best in sports and entertainment, but more importantly, a place where people can spend quality time together, taking away memories they can treasure for a lifetime. On behalf of the City of New York, I offer congratulations and sincere gratitude for 125 years of presenting New Yorkers with the best the world has to offer.

Sincerely,

Michael R. Bloomberg
Mayor

MADISON SQ GARDEN
NATIONAL HORSE SHOW
OPENS TONITE
THRU NEXT TUES
CANADA - GT BRITAIN
UNITED STATES
HAMBURGERS
Nedick's
FRESH FRUIT
ORANGE DRINK
Coca-Cola

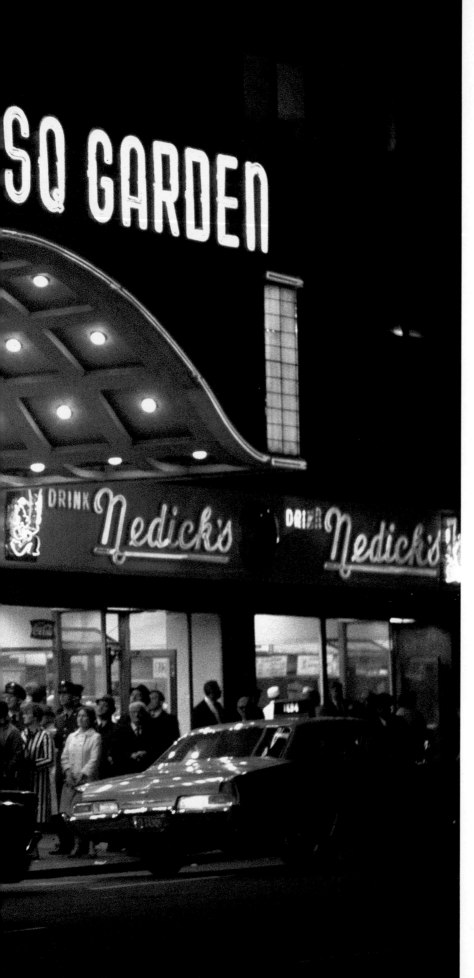

Contents

George Kalinsky Front-Row Seat on History

As official photographer for Madison Square Garden for the past thirty-eight years, I've had the best seat in the house from which to observe and record history in the making. The photo I took of Pope John Paul II holding up a six-year-old girl was seen all over the world. I photographed Willis Reed dramatically limping onto the court to lead the Knicks to their first NBA title, and Mark Messier lifting the Stanley Cup as the Rangers won the NHL championship in 1994, their first in fifty-four years. I've captured the best of the best in track, tennis, college basketball, boxing, gymnastics, and at dog shows.

My job has an eerie component: I never know when I might be taking an historic shot. I recorded John Lennon's final performance before he was shot, and took one of the last photos of John F. Kennedy, Jr., days before his tragic plane crash.

I've also observed the public and private faces of our most renowned personalities. I've seen Judy Garland, looking forlorn and lost in rehearsals and then coming alive onstage; Peggy Fleming, looking carefree and yet in full concentration on the ice; John McEnroe, sometimes intense and focused, at other times volatile and eruptive on the tennis court.

Singers and crooners, rock stars and pop stars, and athletes from all sports, love to perform at the Garden; and I've had the privilege of getting to know many of them. For example, "Ol' Blue Eyes" stopped by my office on March 6, 1971, and asked for assistance: *Life* magazine had asked him to shoot the Muhammad Ali-Joe Frazier fight. After I gave him some photographic tips, we talked about a lot of other things — boxing, art, life, family, even Ava Gardner. We ended up at Patsy's, his favorite restaurant, where he directed the kitchen staff in how to prepare our meal. A week later, Frank Sinatra's photo of the Ali-Frazier fight appeared on the cover of *Life*; thus began a friendship that lasted thirty years.

My life with Madison Square Garden began, strangely enough, on a street corner in Miami, in 1966. I had just graduated from Pratt Institute with a degree in design. While still a student, I had created everything from furniture to the Princess telephone. I used my camera to record my designs, and to take arty or abstract photos of life as I saw it.

The street corner in Miami was where the famous Fifth Street Gym stood. One day as I was strolling past the gym, I saw Muhammad Ali and Howard Cosell walking in. I decided to follow them, but was stopped at the door by Angelo

Dundee, Ali's trainer. I asked Angelo for permission to take a few shots and jokingly told him I was the photographer for Madison Square Garden. The words just came out of my mouth, unplanned, but would turn out to be prophetic.

Dundee was amused. "Why not, Mr. Comedian?" he said. I took twelve shots of Ali training, the first photos I had ever taken of a famous person. That night I heard on the radio that his next championship fight had been canceled; I knew that meant that no other photographer would have access to him for months, while he was in training. I drove to the Miami Herald and asked if they were interested in my film. They developed it and sent a few photos to papers across the country. They were my first photos of a celebrity, and the world got to see them!

Back in New York, I brought my pictures to John F.X. Condon, who was a public relations genius at Madison Square Garden. Handing him my photos, I told John this was the only roll of sports film I had ever taken. He liked them enough to interview me for the role of Garden photographer. As I talked about my background in art and design, it became clear that this was important to him. After listening to my pitch, he said, "If you have the chutzpah to bring me one roll of film, the only roll you have ever taken of any sports action, I have the chutzpah to hire you." I owe my career to him.

I've been honored to be part of the legendary history of Madison Square Garden. In my time, I've been fortunate enough to record moments and events that have had a huge cultural impact on people all over the world. I photographed George Harrison at the Concert for Bangladesh and, thirty years later, Billy Crystal, among many others, at the Concert for New York City. I photographed Wayne Gretzky in his last game, Michael Jordan competing in classic Playoff games against Patrick Ewing and the Knicks, and four political conventions.

From the best show dogs in the world to the most talented gymnasts, from Elvis to Elton, from Barbra to Madonna, from Frank Sinatra to Pope John Paul II, I've captured them all — in a place that truly is "The World's Most Famous Arena."

George Kalinsky

Pete Hamill **The Gardens of New York**

In the country of memory, it is always Friday night and a hard rain is falling on Eighth Avenue. We're coming up from the subway, hundreds of us, and across the avenue, between Forty-ninth and Fiftieth Streets is the Garden. That's all we ever called it.

In that lost night in the 1950s, we're coming from Brooklyn and Queens and the Bronx, from neighborhoods downtown, from Harlem, from Inwood, all the way from New Jersey. The older men are all in overcoats and wearing pearl-gray hats, like the stars of Warner Brothers gangster movies. Many of them have cigars clamped in their jaws. We are hatless in the rain.

We pause under the marquee, smoking, talking, watching, listening. The murmur is constant, an excited buzz, everybody talking about fighters, and among the proper nouns you hear certain names. Robinson. Louis. Marciano. None of whom are fighting on this rain-drowned night, but who live vividly in the dense space under the marquee. We see big shots get out of taxis, in sharp clothes and polished shoes, flicking butts into the rain-slick gutters, and hurry towards the entrance, rushing past the statue of Joe Gans. Some of them have women on their arms who in their blonde glory all look like the B-movie actress Mamie van Doren. Others are alone. Jesus, that's — what's his name, the guy from that quiz show... and there's Al Tisi, remember, the kid fought six rounds underneath last week? And ain't that Tony Janiro? He looks better now than when he was fighting. Yeah, someone says, Graziano fixed his nose... And hey, that's Jimmy Cannon from the *Post*, and there's Dan Parker of the *Mirror*... and, whoa, Tony Canzoneri!

Then we'd go in ourselves, rubbing the Joe Gans bronze for luck, showing the tickets, heading for the balconies and we'd hear the roar before we could see it. Explosive, at a sudden knockdown. Sustained and fierce, when the downed man gets up bleary from hurt and comes back fighting. The glad roar of a packed arena, celebrating heart and will, in those last years when boxing was still a major New York sport.

Later we called it the Old Garden, but in that time it was still just the Garden. I knew it as a young man, and then as a young reporter. On some afternoons, I would visit the offices of the boxing department and talk with Harry Markson or Teddy Brenner, and the visiting managers and trainers, or go down the hall and into the office of *Ring* magazine and chat with Nat Fleischer. The fight mob was the best of company: funny, in a sardonic New York way, at once tough and oddly sentimental. I'd sometimes have a beer at the bar called The Neutral Corner. Or if it was after lunch I'd walk another block uptown and climb the stairs to Stillman's Gym. Or stop in the cafeteria on the east side of Eighth Avenue and have a sandwich across the room from where the gangster Frankie Carbo sipped his coffee with hoodlums who laughed at each of his jokes. Frankie Carbo never laughed. Those places were all part of what we meant when we said those two words: the Garden.

Madison Square Garden was not, of course, an arena reserved for boxing. I saw the circus there as a boy, and the rodeo, on tickets handed out at school. The Rangers played hockey there. I watched the Knicks play basketball there, when the NBA was young, and sat one long afternoon in awe of the stars of track and field. But it was the fight racket that made me come back again and again to the Garden. That, and something else: its connection to the past. There had been a Madison Square Garden for all of my life, and all of my father's life as an immigrant in America. It was the place to which all the men in my neighborhood eventually made a pilgrimage. It stood for continuity and, in its way, for excellence. Only the best ever fought on top at the Garden. Among so many athletes and performers, only the best would ever be remembered.

The photographs by George Kalinsky in this book are aides to memory, because all great photographs freeze time. Through these images we can remember several varieties of reality. Here are those events at which we were witnesses, as fans or reporters. They carry us back into those days or nights when we were joined to thousands of others in a great transcending roar. But they can also make us remember those people and events that we did not see. Here is George Foreman in his first professional prizefight, walking away from a destroyed opponent. Here is a view of the New York Rangers bench, the coach walking in an eerie solitude behind the

OPPOSITE
1967 – Fans arrive for a Rangers game at Garden III.

backs of his players. Such images put us where we had not been. We will now remember the images.

We remember in still another way, because the images evoke the time of our own lives. Who went with us to that Sinatra concert? How old was Elvis that night, and how old was I? Who sat beside us on the night when Muhammad Ali came to do battle with Joe Frazier, and lost, and was not defeated? Fine photographs give us what the French master, Henri Cartier-Bresson, called "the decisive moment." They also give us other things: the moments before, the life that comes later, of the people we watched, and of ourselves.

Many of George Kalinsky's photographs are not about my Garden, the one to which I went while young, but I know that George Kalinsky was in that Old Garden too. He was a boy there. He was a teenager there. He was shaping his talent in that smoky old place, even on nights when he was not armed with a camera. He too sampled the world that I knew. When I first paid my way into the Garden, Eighth Avenue was already in full decline, a jumble of sex shops, porno movies, seedy bars, and a floating population of streetwalkers and junkies. Not many of them bothered the fight crowd. Even towards the end, when it was even shabbier, and the big fights had all fled to Las Vegas, the Garden, in its rough way, symbolized the survival of a simpler New York past. There were men in those audiences who had survived the speakeasies of Prohibition, or had come through the terrible time of the Depression, or had fought World War II. Nothing much intimidated them. When they talked about "moxie," in prizefighting or in life, they knew what it was. They didn't talk tough. They were tough. They remembered good times and bad. There were even a few of them who remembered another Garden, one that actually stood, twenty-nine blocks away, on Madison Square.

The green urban oasis called Madison Square contains about six acres between Madison and Fifth Avenues and Twenty-third and Twenty-sixth Streets. Originally a much larger parade ground for militia soldiers, it was reduced to its present size in 1845, then leveled and landscaped, with paths added and a fence erected to keep out roaming pigs, and opened as a park in 1847. The place where the first Garden was built was just above Twenty-sixth Street on the east side of Madison Avenue. It was a mess of stables and loading platforms built for Commodore Vanderbilt's railroad, which was not allowed to bring steam engines south of Forty-second Street and had to use horses to haul the cars to the depot. When Vanderbilt finished the early version of Grand

Central Terminal in 1871, the yard was essentially abandoned. A few early promoters used the site for shows, without much success.

In stepped an extraordinary New Yorker named P.T. Barnum. He was the greatest showman in New York history, equipped with audacity, a sense of popular taste, great intelligence, and a gambler's instincts. He looked at this empty lot and saw gold. In 1873, he leased the depot to mount his "Monster Classical and Geological Hippodrome." He walled off the area, pitched a huge tent in the open area, and persuaded 15,000 New Yorkers to pay a dollar each to see an array of tumblers, jugglers, Arabian horses, cowboys and Indians, and tattooed men. The crowds added further vitality to the restaurants around Madison Square, and to the theaters that were opening all along Twenty-third Street.

The trouble was the New York weather. Barnum did good business in the warm months, but none of the buildings at the old depot were heated, and no shows could be mounted there during the ferocious New York winters. In 1874, the lease passed to a musician and promoter named Patrick Gilmore, who that summer booked a slew of temperance lectures, beauty contests, and flower shows, and called the place Gilmore's Garden. He landscaped the grounds. He gave band concerts, with himself as leader. And he created the first Westminster Kennel Club Dog Show. The big money did not come. Again the lease changed hands, a year after the death of the Commodore. And then Vanderbilt's son and heir, William K. Vanderbilt, thought he could make the site into a good thing. He conceived of the place as a venue for sporting events, added a story to the Madison Avenue façade, and gave the place its new name: Madison Square Garden.

A few months later, the façade of that wing collapsed, killing three people and injuring twenty-two. But no substantial changes were made in the drafty old building. Barnum returned with the circus. Vanderbilt booked six-day bike races and exhibitions of boxing (the sport was then banned in New York State but he used the likes of John L. Sullivan to give "instructional" exhibitions). In 1883, the Garden became the official site of the National Horse Show. Still, during most of the winters, it was an empty walled tundra. In 1887, Vanderbilt sold out to a group of men who planned to tear down the existing structure and build a new, all-year-round Madison Square Garden. The syndicate of investors included J.P. Morgan, one of the richest men in America, and a brilliant young architect named Stanford White.

When White was asked to design the new Garden in 1888, he was thirty-five years old, tall (six-three), with red hair, a dashing manner, enormous energy, and an easy brilliance. He also had a reputation for his affairs with young women. He was married, lived with his wife and young son in Gramercy Park, but kept his own hours. As was true of many men of his time and class, most of White's affairs were sexual, rather than romantic; there were few long-term relationships, no woman for whom he would break up his marriage. He just loved women and was not the first man in history to behave with women like a knave or a fool. But that part of his reputation was usually brushed aside because of the immense size of his talent.

In 1888, he was the star of the great architectural firm of McKim, Mead and White, whose Broadway offices would soon be located just below Twenty-third Street. White was a gifted draftsman, a man of devouring eclecticism, his restless mind plundering the architectural treasures of Europe for ideas that could be converted into architectural grandeur in New York. Many of his buildings exist to this day as an essential component of the city's look and style. For many months after being given the commission for the new Garden, White poured all of his enormous energy into the new complex, as if determined to create a masterpiece. He did.

The opening took place on the evening of June 16, 1890, and the crowd included Civil War general William T. Sherman, the vice-president of the United States, Levi P. Morton, and twelve thousand members of the city's social elite or those who aspired to be part of it. What they saw was stunning. As White's biographer, Paul R. Baker, described it in *Stanny: The Gilded Life of Stanford White*:

"From the principal entrance on Madison Avenue, the first-nighters moved through a long entrance lobby lined with polished yellow Siena marble, emerging into the huge and colorful amphitheater, said to be the largest such arena in the United States. Gold and white terra cotta tiles, rather than

yellow as originally suggested, decorated most interior walls, with some surfaces painted pale red. Two tiers of seats rose along the sides, and three tiers of boxes, trimmed in maroon plush, filled the ends of the vast room. Some 10,000 spectators could be seated comfortably in the amphitheater, and there was standing room or, for some events, floor seating for up to 4,000 more. An upper-level promenade, well utilized for strolling, gazing, and visiting, extended around the circuit of the arena. The high roof was spectacularly supported by twenty-eight large columns, with exposed steel trusses, lined with incandescent lights, reaching about 180 feet from side to side. At the center of the roof, an enormous skylight could, as if by magic, be rolled aside by machinery. This was done during the opening performance, but it occurred so quietly that most spectators were not even aware of the change until they noticed the cool night air. As in ancient arenas, provision was made for flooding the floor for water spectacles. As at the Roman Colosseum, animal stables to be used for the horse shows and circus performances were placed in the basement below. Here was a bit of ancient Rome, transformed, modernized, and brought to Gilded Age New York!"

The luxurious amphitheater was only part of the complex. There was a theater with twelve hundred seats, and a splendid restaurant, and a concert hall. And above all, there was the tower. White drew his inspiration from the 275-foot tower of the cathedral in Seville (and the architecture in general was in a Spanish Renaissance style). His tower rose 320 feet into the empty New York sky, from the base of the main building to the pinnacle, with an interior elevator shaft and circular staircase climbing to a roof garden. On the lower part of the tower, White designed seven floors of small apartments (he would take one for himself), and at the top, he asked his friend Augustus (Gus) Saint-Gaudens to create a statue of Diana the Huntress that would revolve on a special ball-bearing base, aiming an arrow at all parts of New York. The naked goddess was a sensation in prim New York. But the first version was too large, ruining the proportions of the finished tower. The two friends removed it at their own expense, and replaced it with a smaller Diana. White had his masterpiece.

The story did not end there. The new Madison Square Garden was not a financial success. It had cost $3,000,000 (ten times that amount in today's money). The monthly operating "nut" was about $20,000. In addition, most of the theaters of Twenty-third Street were heading north to what would become Times Square. But, still, the Garden was the Garden. It went on. So did Stanford White. At some point in 1901, he met a beautiful sixteen-year-old named Evelyn Nesbit. That part of his story has been told in all the White biographies, in E.L. Doctorow's wonderful

"The Garden is 'one of the great institutions of the town, to be mentioned along with Central Park and the bridge of Brooklyn.'"

— *NEW YORK TIMES*, 1890

novel *Ragtime*, in such movies as *The Girl on the Red Velvet Swing*. It led to one of the most lurid scandals in the city's history. As usual, jealousy was the heart of the matter. After White ended his affair with Nesbit, she went on to marry a rich, and disturbed, young man named Harry Thaw. She told him about White, perhaps to provoke his jealousy. Thaw became obsessed with the architect, although his wife's affair with White had long ago turned to ashes. The ashes still contained some embers — for Thaw. On the night of June 25th, 1906, Thaw and his wife were in the rear of the roof garden restaurant of Madison Square Garden, where a show called *Mamzelle Champagne* was playing. Three friends were with them. White, an investor in the show, sat alone at a table near the stage and both Thaw and Nesbit noted his presence. Around 11 o'clock, Thaw and his party got up to leave. Then Thaw, wearing a long coat and a tuxedo in spite of the warm June heat, returned alone. Witnesses remembered that he looked calm and deliberate. He walked up to White and shot him three times in the head, killing him instantly.

The aftermath was almost as ugly as the murder. The free-spending White turned out to be virtually bankrupt, and his partners struggled to console his widow, and arrange some financial stability for the family. The newspapers (and Thaw's lawyers) put the murdered man on trial, accusing White of being a voluptuary, a sexual pervert, an arrogant defiler of young women, implying that he got what he deserved. With a few exceptions (the great journalist Richard Harding Davis was one of them) none of his friends publicly defended him against the furious storm of sanctimony and hypocrisy. After one hung jury, Thaw was eventually found innocent by reason of insanity, spent some years in the upstate Matteawan Hospital for the Criminally Insane, escaped briefly to Canada, was caught, recommitted, and released at last in 1915. He then divorced Evelyn and, like the rich people in F. Scott Fitzgerald's *The Great Gatsby*, retreated into his money. Poor Evelyn Nesbit had peddled her story in vaudeville houses, then retreated into booze and drugs. Thaw died in Miami in 1947. Nesbit died in Los Angeles in 1967.

By the time of Thaw's final acquittal, Madison Square Garden had grown shabby, gone through several new owners, then fallen into bankruptcy in 1916. The New York Life Insurance Company held the Garden's $2,300,000 mortgage. World War I prevented the company from doing much with their white elephant, and, for a while, the advent of Prohibition meant bad days for many parts of the entertainment business that depended upon the sale of booze. Most journalists suspected that New York Life would just tear the place down and do what others were doing all over the city: put up an office building. But in the face of public uproar over destruction of the Garden, the insurance company hesitated. Then the Garden assumed a new, very short lease on life.

"Madison Square Garden is, 'Not a building, but a state of mind.'"

— *HERALD TRIBUNE EDITORIAL*, 1925

ABOVE
Promoter and Garden impresario Tex Rickard between Luis Firpo (L) and Jack Dempsey (R) prior to their 1923 heavyweight title fight at Garden II.

The unwritten terms of the lease had two parts. One was the passage in 1920 of the Walker Law — sponsored by the charming rogue who would later be Mayor, a state legislator named Jimmy Walker. This legalized boxing, which in multi-ethnic New York was to become a major sport, as Jews were matched with Irishmen and the winners fought Italian-Americans. The other part of the temporary respite from extinction was the arrival in New York of the great boxing promoter Tex Rickard, a man P.T. Barnum would have loved.

Rickard had staged one hugely successful fight under the old Frawley Law (no knockdowns, no official decisions), matching Jess Willard against Frank Moran. That 1916 fight was won by Willard and brought in $152,000, the largest single gate in the history of the Garden to date. Then the Walker Law passed. Rickard was already the promoter of the heavyweight champion of the world, a fierce puncher named Jack Dempsey, who had taken the title from Willard in 1919 in Toledo. Then, as now, the man who controlled the heavyweight champion usually controlled boxing.

Rickard signed a lease for ten years with New York Life, spent $200,000 to spruce up the place, and went to work. He brought the best fighters back to New York, but he knew that prizefighting alone would never be enough. He devised a plan to fill seats with every conceivable kind of entertainment. He often filled the house with the circus, the dog show, the horse show, various charity events, and then, in 1924, he attracted the Democratic National Convention. He landed this hilarious form of entertainment by offering the Garden rent-free to the Democrats. He knew a great show when he saw one. But he had no way of knowing that it would be the longest such convention in history, the delegates going to 103 ballots over sixteen days before settling on one John W. Davis, who was flattened in the general election by Calvin Coolidge. At that moment in the saga of the Garden, Rickard was already on his way out the door. New York Life was at last ready to build its office building. Rickard had already chosen to build a new arena, with the backing of a number of investors. This new arena would be on Eighth Avenue, way uptown, and Rickard cheerfully ignored geography and named it Madison Square Garden.

The last fight at the old arena took place on May 5, 1925, matching the lightweights Sid Terris and Johnny Dundee. The place was packed and brimming with nostalgia and a sense of loss. Jimmy Walker and Jack Dempsey were at ringside. Terris won a decision, and then the Madison Square Garden of Stanford White was dead, aged 35.

There could not have been a better time for Rickard to take the Garden uptown. The town of New York was the capital city of what columnist Westbrook Pegler would call "The Era of Wonderful Nonsense." The city was throbbing with energy, from the booming stock market and from the explosion of big-time sports whose engine in New York was a New York Yankee named Babe Ruth. Great energy also came from the booming underworld. Prohibition was already a preposterous failure, a triumph of boondocks religious nuts (and some feminists) over common sense. New Yorkers had been drinking, smoking, and wenching since the time of the Dutch. They would not stop because some idealistic, moralizing fools had passed a law. After two years of the Great Experiment, New York's 15,000 shuttered drinking establishments had been replaced by 30,000 speakeasies. "Prohibition," said Ziegfeld Follies star Will Rogers, "is better than no drinking at all." Many immigrants and their children believed that the law was aimed directly at them, and thus felt it was their patriotic duty as Americans to defy it.

Some defied it in a professional way. Prohibition created the Mob, that coalition of Irish, Jewish, and Italian gangsters that would survive, in various forms, for almost seven decades. As bootleggers and rum runners, the Mob guys were, of course, technically criminals. But they were giving the people what they wanted, and in the New York imagination, the bootlegger functioned as a kind of defiant romantic hero. In the same year that the third Garden opened, Fitzgerald published *The Great Gatsby*, which perfectly captured the romantic allure of the bootlegger.

The new gangsters — most of them young — all loved sports, and the chance to gamble on contests and games. Most of them lived in greater Times Square, patronized its restaurants and clubs, and for them the new Garden was an essential part of their lives, a kind of neighborhood playground. It was a permanent part of the geography of that glittering Broadway that Damon Runyon would sentimentalize, and Mark Hellinger would see with more knowing eyes, the place that seemed in memory to have a soundtrack spoken by Walter Winchell. After 1919, Joseph M. Patterson's exuberant new tabloid, the *Daily News*, made that Broadway a permanent beat. Babe Ruth moved through that Broadway. Jack Dempsey would open several restaurants there. Al Jolson was its reigning show business prince, playing at the Winter Garden Theater, and Fanny Brice its princess, right down there at The Palace. And there was Arnold Rothstein, the most powerful of all New York gamblers, sitting at his personal table in the new place on Broadway near Fiftieth Street called Lindy's, while wise guys whispered that he was the man who had fixed the 1919 World Series. They didn't say it to his face (Rothstein would appear in Fitzgerald's novel as the gambler Meyer Wolfsheim). There, too, were Owney Madden, and Larry Fay, and Legs Diamond, tough guys all, some of them smart, a few of them murderous gunsels. And right there, coming out of her own joint, was the exuberant queen of the speakeasies, Miss Texas Guinan.

All of them gambled, and the worst would gamble on anything: the color of socks on the next guy to come around the corner, the first of a bank of elevators to reach the top of an office building, the girl from the Ziegfeld Follies who would sleep with one of three wise guys. They studied racing charts as if they were composed by alchemists who could turn lead into gold. At the Garden they would gamble on six-day bike races or indoor soccer or the order of march of the Coldstream Guards. But boxing was what got their most sustained patronage, since there was no horseracing anywhere in the neighborhood. They hung out in gyms. They bought pieces of fighters. They tried to fix fights, and sometimes did. At one point, hoodlums owned Primo Carnera, who became, briefly, the heavyweight champion of the world. Mob guys being Mob guys, they often lied, and pretended to have control of fighters who were actually honest. Their presence permeated the game.

All of that time remained in the building when I first started going there and the images were all in black and white, like those movies called film noir. The ghosts of the great fighters were there: Benny Leonard and Jimmy McLarnin, Mickey Walker and Barney Ross and Henry Armstrong along with Beau Jack and Willie Pep and Sandy Saddler and, and… everybody had his own list, all of them made imaginary matches, all called upon memory that was often just a legend passed down from their fathers.

OPPOSITE
The hot dog stand inside the main lobby of
Garden III was a popular gathering spot.

When Rickard opened the "new" Garden in 1925, hockey was brought to New Yorkers. The New York Americans played at the Garden during the winter of 1925-1926, renting the arena for their home games. Rickard and his associates decided to launch their own team, and the New York Rangers, for Tex's Rangers, were born.

But in those years after World War II there was something else rising in the Garden: the city game. The first draft of the National Basketball Association started in 1946, and the New York team was called the Knickerbockers. When I was a boy, nobody cared much about the Knicks. Basketball was a college game and in our blue-collar neighborhood, like most of the city's neighborhoods, very few people finished high school. We were Dodger fans where I lived, just as Manhattan kids were Giant fans, and Bronx kids were Yankee fans (with a number of exceptions in all boroughs). There was no television, so we had to go to the ballpark to see the game at its best. And we played similar games: stickball, baseball, and softball (sometimes called "indoor"). Our other sport was boxing, and some of us went to the gyms of the Police Athletic League or the local schools and tried to learn the fundamentals. Along came basketball.

Two events drove basketball deeper into our consciousness. One was the triumph in the mid-1950s of television. For the first time, many kids could actually see how the game was supposed to be played. The other was the departure in 1957 of the Brooklyn Dodgers and New York Giants to the gold fields of California. The bitterness over that combined loss made many New Yorkers give up on baseball for a very long time. Their need to follow a team, to root for triumph in spite of defeat and disappointment, drew them to basketball. Television educated them in the nuances of the game. They didn't need instruction about the game's speed and grace. In the early 1960s, you began to see kids in playgrounds all over the city. They were playing basketball. It had become the city game.

Two other changes were also taking place. One was prosperity. When World War II ended so did a fifteen-year period of sacrifice and deprivation that included the Depression. Poor kids who once chose to become prizefighters suddenly found themselves with jobs. Many of them bought automobiles. Suddenly one summer there was no room on the "court" of the street to play stickball. Basketball was safe behind the fences of playgrounds. The player need not fear being run over by a new Buick when a ball went out of bounds. And as kids' baseball got more organized, with the horrors of Little Leagues quickly erasing all the careless joy of the game, baseball became very expensive to play. Gloves, spikes, batting gloves, uniforms: all cost money. In the playground, poor kids only needed one ball and a basket. Basketball became for city kids what soccer was in all the poor countries of the planet.

The other great shift was caused by the G.I. Bill of Rights, the most important piece of social legislation since the New Deal. For the first time, the sons and daughters of factory workers and longshoremen and taxi drivers had a chance to go to the university. They took the chance, and changed America with their intelligence and creativity and capacity for work. Too many of them, alas, took the low-cost mortgages for veterans and moved to the suburbs, far from the energizing streets, far from Madison Square Garden.

Their kids followed the Knicks on television, and on special occasions — a birthday, a graduation — they went into the city to see a game at the Garden. They would remember such nights all of their lives. But the parents were wary of Eighth Avenue, of the sullen presence of heroin and menace. The Garden, to many of them, felt like a symbol of decay. They rushed home to the suburbs. The Garden management saw what was happening in the squalid slum of Eighth Avenue. They started laying plans for the fourth Garden.

The new Garden was built on the scene of the destruction of Pennsylvania Station. Literally millions of New Yorkers had grown up with Penn Station, had met their husbands, wives or lovers in the Waiting Room, had departed on trips that changed their lives, had returned there from distant places, including wars, to the good place they called home. This was not a question of sentimentality or empty nostalgia. The station created deep, ineradicable emotions. But there was something else about it: the old Penn Station was one of the most extraordinary buildings ever erected in New York, or anywhere else. Again, Stanford White is part of the story.

The idea for Penn Station began in 1901, and a year later McKim, Mead and White were charged with the design. To link the mainland to Manhattan, tunnels would cut under the Hudson River to the site in the notorious old Tenderloin district. The new station would occupy two city blocks from Seventh to Eighth Avenues, between Thirty-first and Thirty-third Streets, a total of eight acres. The site was cleared, with thousands of New Yorkers — including many African-Americans — forced to move, some going as far away as Harlem. The fine American artist George Bellows made several paintings of the site, as the deep digging got under way; they now bear an eerie resemblance to the World Trade Center site after September 11, 2001. Then the building went up. There had been nothing like it in the city's history. The exterior featured gray granite Doric columns based on Bernini's design for the plaza in front of St. Peter's in Rome. The interior Waiting Room was designed as a variation on the Baths of Caracalla, the largest structure in ancient Rome. Charles McKim was the primary architect, but White was part of the design process until his murder in 1906. He never saw the completed building.

The original discussion of a new Garden on the site of Pennsylvania Station started in 1960 between officials of the Garden Corporation and the railroad, and at first the public talk was about "air rights" over the terminal. The plan contained a certain logic. After all, what could be a better location? The Long Island Railroad could quickly carry many of those suburbanites to the new Garden, as could the trains of Penn Central. The two major subway lines connected to the site could deliver most New Yorkers. Soon, "air rights" vanished from the discussion. The word now was a blunt as an axe: the best, most efficient way to make this all happen would be to destroy Penn Station and build a new Garden on the ruins.

There were huge public protests against what many New Yorkers saw as an act of municipal vandalism. They got nowhere. This was a real estate deal, and Penn Station belonged to a private corporation. The assault on the building started on October 28, 1963. I was working in Europe that year. When I returned in the fall of 1964, the old station was gone. Unlike most New Yorkers, I never got a chance to say goodbye.

In 1965, as a result of the destruction of Penn Station, the Landmarks Preservation Commission was formed, with full legal powers to save the historic buildings of New York. It was too late to preserve Pennsylvania Station. But what happened to Pennsylvania Station would never be allowed to happen again.

The new Garden opened for business on February 11, 1968, while the government in Washington was reeling from the late January shock of the Tet Offensive in Vietnam. Three nights later, the Knicks played San Diego and Walt Frazier scored the New York team's first two points. In the end, as these selected photographs remind us, few fans cared about the architecture. They went to see what was in the building itself. And here came the Knicks of Frazier and Reed and Bradley and DeBusschere, roaring to their first ever NBA championship in 1970. Here to the new Garden came Muhammad Ali and Joe Frazier and every other great fighter of the times, most competing to capture the attention of old men with frozen memories, all of them in black and white, the colors of ghosts.

Hey, he's good, says a guy coming down the ramp. But he ain't Ray Robinson.

Who the hell ever was? says his friend.

Robinson was, says the first guy.

The new fighters were in the Garden, but so was Robinson and Louis and Zivic and Gavilan and all the others. Memory had traveled downtown too. But boxing was not all, it wasn't even close, not in the Garden of the Knicks and the Rangers, not as the sixties moved into the seventies, when the Knicks won two World Championships, the eighties and then the nineties, which saw a citywide celebration as the Rangers won the Stanley Cup, and saw the introduction of a new team to the Garden, the Liberty of the WNBA, rolling to the end of the century. Here, too, came arena rock and roll: the Rolling Stones, John Lennon, Bob Dylan, Bruce Springsteen, George Harrison, Eric Clapton, the Grateful Dead, Madonna, U2, and all the other artists of the times, decade after decade. Here were the amazing salsa concerts, packed to the roof, of

the Fania All-Stars. Right there, in the ring, that was Frank Sinatra. And that singer from Brooklyn was Barbra Streisand. And next week...

So I kept going to the Garden, in spite of my feelings about the way it was built and the way it looked from the sidewalk. I went as a newspaperman. I went as a fan. I went as a father. I went because it was the place where the greatest of all performers came to show the world what they were made of, in their time and mine. I still go to the Garden, and will keep going as long as there is breath in my body. Like every other fan, I go in hopes of being astonished. Usually, I'm not. That is true of life too, of course. But sometimes the magic comes, as it did with Michael Jordan in the seasons of his prime. Sometimes the magic comes to beat the team you love, but that doesn't diminish the great power of the magic. Then, almost as quickly as he arrived, even a transcendent magician like Jordan is gone. You are sure his likes will not come this way again. And still you go, hoping to be astonished, to be taken out of yourself, to be lifted beyond the ordinary and the mundane to a new place. These days, in a world more dangerous than ever, where fanatics want so desperately to affirm belief by spilling blood, I think a lot about my grandson, who, as I write, is almost six. Soon I will tell him about Ray Robinson. Soon I will try to explain Michael Jordan and Willis Reed and Walt Frazier and Patrick Ewing and Rod Gilbert and Mark Messier and about leaving it all on the floor. I will try to explain Sinatra, too, and Streisand and Dylan and Celia Cruz. I will try to explain magic.

And with any luck, that boy will carry the legends with him on some night of hard rain and come out of the subway and enter the Garden, wherever it may be, and be astonished. Even if I'm not with him, I'll be there too.

OPPOSITE
The fourth Garden has stood between Thirty-first and Thirty-third Streets and Seventh and Eighth Avenues since 1968.

BOXING

"That block-long Garden was by far the best. It was the center of sports life and entertainment in New York."

– JACK DEMPSEY

PREVIOUS SPREAD
April 25, 1966 – Emile Griffith takes on Dick Tiger for the middleweight championship and wins in a 15-round decision.

BOTTOM
February 23, 1945 – Sugar Ray Robinson on his way to defeating Jake LaMotta in a 10-round unanimous decision in front of a sellout crowd of 18,000 fans.

TOP
December 14, 1920 – Jack Dempsey (R) fought Bill Brennan (L) in a heavyweight title bout at Garden II in front of 16,948 fans. Dempsey knocked out Brennan in the twelfth round to retain his title.

February 11, 1949 – Sandy Saddler (R) and Willie Pep fought for the world featherweight title in what *The Ring* magazine called the fight of the year. Pep won in a 15-round unanimous decision, retaining his title.

October 26, 1951 – In what would be his last fight, Joe Louis (L) got knocked down by Rocky Marciano (R). Louis fought an amazing seventy-one bouts, including seven successful title defenses at the Garden.

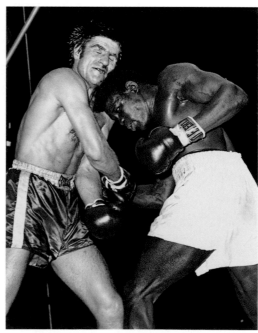

BELOW LEFT
February 1968 – Buster Mathis, in training prior to his bout with Joe Frazier.

TOP
March 13, 1963 – Cassius Clay (Muhammad Ali) defeated Doug Jones (L) in a 10-round unanimous decision.

BELOW RIGHT
March 4, 1968 – Joe Frazier (R) takes on Buster Mathis (L) in the first boxing card at Garden IV, defeating Mathis by KO in the eleventh round.

ABOVE
Muhammad Ali

ABOVE
Joe Frazier

George Foreman

The Fight of the Century

They were wearing big fur coats, high boots, lavish outfits and hairdos: and we haven't even described the ladies yet...those were the men!

It was March 8, 1971, Madison Square Garden, and two undefeated heavyweights were fighting for the championship of the world. This match wasn't just a fight; it was a battle between two classic heavyweights who were larger than life. It was the only place in the world to be that night. Never before or since has there been a night like that. And be assured this was not about the money: it was all about "being there."

There were Frank Sinatra, photographing ringside, Burt Lancaster broadcasting, and LeRoy Neiman sketching the scene. Also at ringside were Diana Ross, sitting with Garden boss Alvin Cooperman, fight promoter Jerry Perenchio, Sammy Davis Jr., Peter Falk, James Taylor, Walt "Clyde" Frazier, and "Broadway Joe" Namath. They came from all over the world; I saw Prince Rainier, Leonard Bernstein, and my hero Joe Louis, with Vegas casino boss Ash Resnic. I was thrilled to be sitting ringside.

"Every fan, every person was a celebrity, and a part of history. Never before had two undefeated champions fought."

Every person in the Garden that night felt important because it was that kind of night. Every fan, every person was a celebrity, and a part of history. Never before had two undefeated champions fought. As the bell sounded, the ring announcer, Johnny Addie — in his made-for-the-moment, classy way — introduced the two evenly-matched champions. There was suspense as we wondered how he would introduce Muhammad Ali, who had not fought a championship fight in more than two years, while taking a stand against the Vietnam War.

When the fight started, the Garden was electric. People started shouting for Joe Frazier, who was the house fighter — a fact many fans do not know. Round after round you thought one of them was going to win, only to see the other one come back.

They were pretty even until the thirteenth round. Then Ali got knocked down in the middle of the ring, and I can still see Ali's corner man, Drew Bundini, throwing a pail of water that hit him square on the money, just like a baseball to the head. This was against the rules, and I had never seen that before. It did revive Ali, but this was Joe Frazier's night. He conquered Mt. Everest.

There is a boxing expression that goes, "Put your head on your man," meaning you put your head on his chest and keep it there all night. But no one ever does it, it's just an expression. However, in the last two rounds of this epic fight Joe did it, controlling Ali by rolling his head and moving him left and right. I had never witnessed that before.

OPPOSITE
February 1971 – Muhammad Ali met Joe Frazier for
the first time prior to the "Fight of the Century."

TRAINING HDQTS.
FOR JOE FRAZIER
HEAVYWEIGHT
CHAMPION

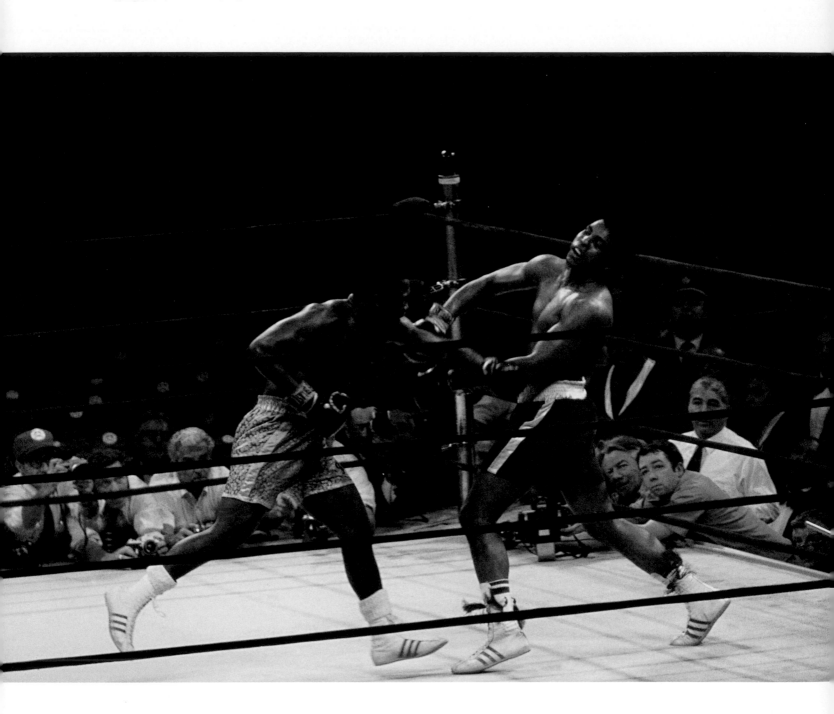

On that night, Muhammad Ali was the most vanquished boxer I've ever seen. I also knew Joe Frazier would never be the same again. In winning, Joe took a huge pounding himself. He would never quite be the same either, and there would never be a night to top this one. This was Joe's moment, this was Joe's time, this was the night Joe Frazier climbed the mountain — and it could only be accomplished in Madison Square Garden. It simply could not have happened anywhere else.

When I fought Joe for the title two years later, in Jamaica, I knocked him down to win the heavyweight championship of the world. But he wasn't the same Joe Frazier. I was waving the American flag in victory, but I felt so bad, because you didn't want to see Joe Frazier lose. I love the man.

Joe Frazier and Muhammad Ali are joined at the hip; I cannot visualize one without the other. They were the first fighters who brought celebrity to boxing, which started on that March night in 1971, with the "Fight of the Century" — that historic fight at the Garden. They paved the way for other fighters, like me, to achieve success and a high-profile celebrity status. When I'm doing a commercial, I am more proud that it happened for George Foreman the boxer, and for boxing, than for myself.

I will never forget that first Ali-Frazier fight at the Garden, and how each fighter looked like they had battled in a war as the bell sounded, ending the final round. It was the toughest-fought fifteen rounds you will ever see. And while Joe Frazier won the fight, there were no losers at the Garden that night.

One last thought: if I had to be in a foxhole, Muhammad Ali would be my overwhelming first choice for the person to have in there with me. He is the greatest, and he would never give up; he would fight to the end. What a hero he is!

OPPOSITE
March 8, 1971 – "The Fight of the Century." In the first heavyweight title bout between two undefeated champions, Joe Frazier defeated Muhammad Ali in a hard-fought 15-round decision.

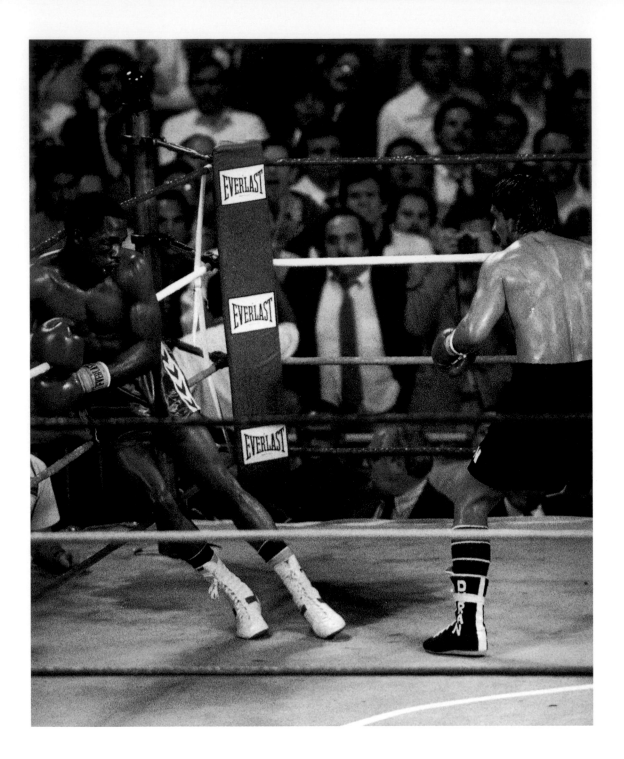

ABOVE

June 23, 1969 – George Foreman, after he defeated
Don Waldhelm in a third round KO. This was Foreman's
first professional fight, coming off his 1968 Olympic
gold medal victory.

Michael J. Fox

Boxing at the Garden

Growing up in Canada, where hockey transcends pastime and verges on religion, I was aware of the Rangers, and where they played their home games. Madison Square Garden fired my young imagination for an entirely different reason, though. It was the Mecca of professional boxing; a sport far more exciting and exotic than the shinny played every winter's day on the local pond.

If I had my own time-traveling DeLorean I'd take multiple trips back to the Garden of the 1940s, 50s, 60s, and 70s, when fighters like Joe Louis, Rocky Marciano, Sugar Ray Robinson, Floyd Patterson, Joe Frazier, and Muhammad Ali were in their glory. Of course, knowing the outcomes as I do I might be tempted to place a few bets, but that's beside the point. There is simply no event more electrifying than two gritty warriors slugging it out for the championship of the world.

"I figured that watching the heavyweight championship of the world at Madison Square Garden must be like touching the face of God — well beyond my reach."

Of the many legendary Garden title bouts, the war between the two undefeated heavyweights Joe Frazier and Muhammad Ali truly deserves its "Fight of the Century" designation. I was ten years old at the time and, along with my older brother Steve, sat transfixed as we watched it on TV. We would catch all the big fights and then run down to the basement, wrap our fists in hockey elbow pads, and re-enact the highlights. Unfortunately, in the Fox brothers' version of "Ali–Frazier," I played Ali, and so, despite a valiant effort, took a beating. I would have given anything to be at the Garden that night, not just to witness the fight itself, but also the spectacle: all the famous actors and athletes sitting ringside, decked out in their furs, jewels, and feather boas — and that was just the men. It was mesmerizing. I figured that watching the heavyweight championship of the world at Madison Square Garden must be like touching the face of God — well beyond my reach.

The 1970s and 80s brought a transition into an era of great welter and middleweights — Sugar Ray Leonard, Roberto Duran, Tommy Hearns, and Marvin Hagler. During these years my life changed too. I became an actor and left Canada for the States, eventually moving to New York City. Still a boxing devotee, I had gone from watching the fights on TV to having choice seats at the Garden, from being a fan of Duran's to getting a bear hug from him ringside. Here, all around me, were the storied characters of the New York boxing scene, walking, talking, cheering, and chomping unlit cigars. Jake LaMotta cracked jokes, Bud Schulberg and George Plimpton swapped stories, and LeRoy Neiman recorded it all for posterity on his sketchpad. There's no crowd like a fight crowd, and the crowd at the Garden is a universe unto itself.

This proved especially true on March 13, 1999. The Evander Holyfield-Lennox Lewis heavyweight title bout at the Garden buzzed with celebrities. In my section alone sat Michael Douglas, Jack Nicholson, John F. Kennedy, Jr., Joe Frazier, Spike Lee, and many others; more boldface names than on Page Six of the *New York Post*.

OPPOSITE
March 13, 1999 – Evander Holyfield and Lennox Lewis fought to a disputed 15-round draw in their world championship heavyweight title bout.

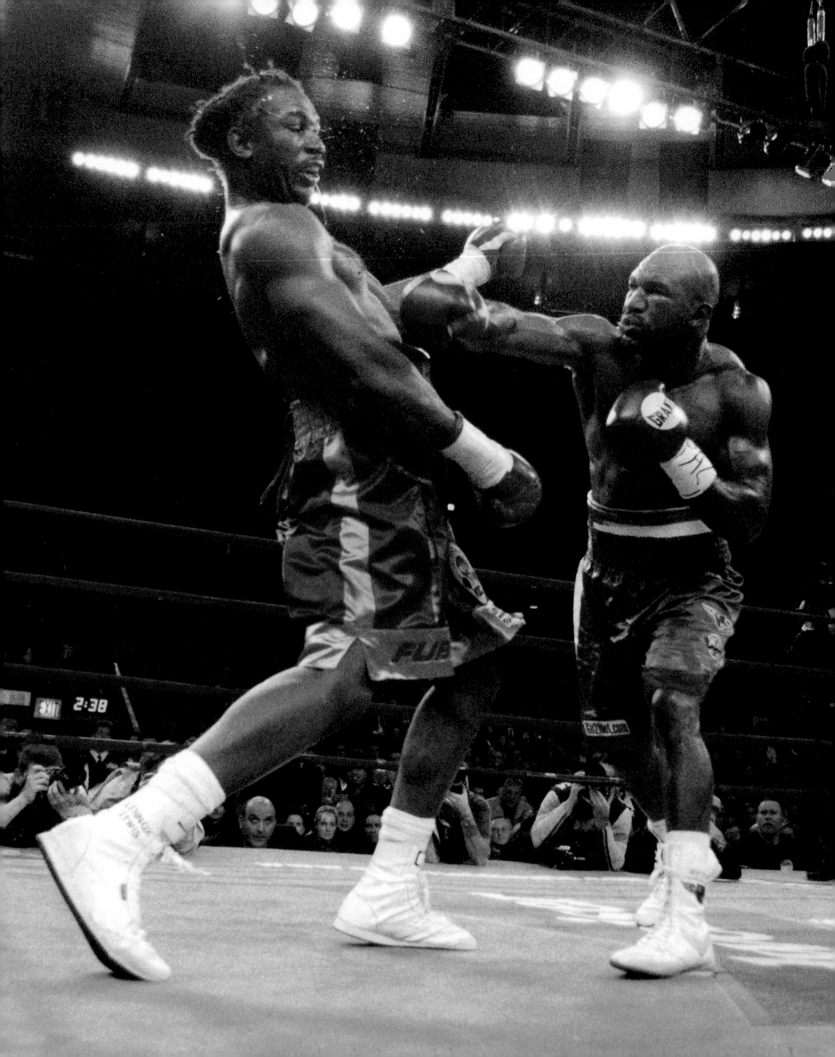

ABOVE
January 26, 2002 – Vernon Forrest celebrated after
he defeated "Sugar" Shane Mosley to capture the WBC
welterweight title in a 12-round unanimous decision.

"You're happy to get the opportunity to fight here. . . that's how you become part of what they call history."

– EVANDER HOLYFIELD

On this night, though, they were all boxing fans first, intensely focused on the main event. With the fight close (it would end in a controversial draw), the crowd became increasingly vocal. From behind me, someone with a British accent was loudly supporting his countryman Lewis. I turned around to see Keith Richards. That was cool enough, but I did a double-take when I realized that, sitting next to Keith was John McCain. Only at a boxing match can you see the pirate king of the Rolling Stones alongside a Republican Senator of Arizona, both just loving the fight. At that moment there was nowhere else on the planet that I would rather have been. A childhood fantasy had been made real.

I have attended other memorable fight-nights at the Garden, like September 29, 2001 when Bernard Hopkins pounded the favored Felix Trinidad to win the undisputed middleweight championship, unifying the WBC, WBA, and IBF belts. But my important Madison Square Garden experiences are not limited to sports. I've seen the Rolling Stones, U2, and Pearl Jam play to packed houses, and was privileged to be a part of the Concert for New York City. That concert showed what the Garden means to New York and the world. After the shock and grief of September 11th, it provided a most appropriate place for everyone to come together, feel a sense of community, and support New York City's police, firefighters, emergency service personnel, and their families. It was a night of recovery and a time for all to gather up the courage to battle on. After all, Madison Square Garden has long been a showcase for fighters, and the fighting spirit.

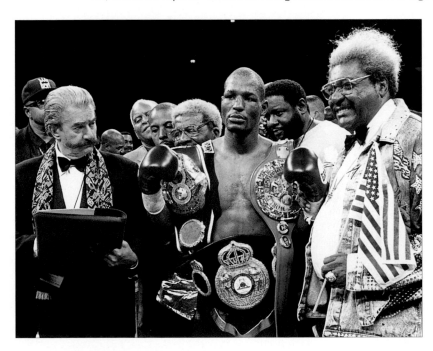

ABOVE
September 29, 2001 – Bernard Hopkins with the WBC, WBA, and IBF belts after he defeated Felix Trinidad to win the combined middleweight world championship. With Hopkins are LeRoy Neiman (L) and Don King (R).

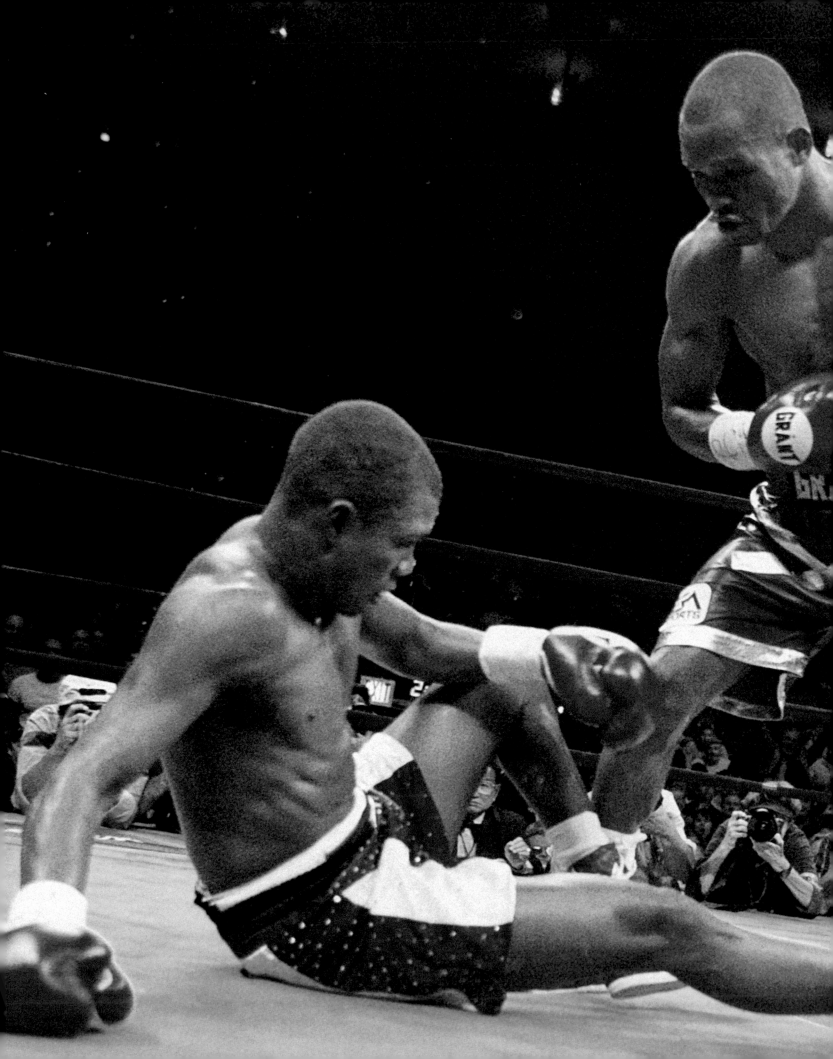

LEFT
September 29, 2001 – Bernard Hopkins towered over Felix Trinidad in the twelfth round; Hopkins won the fight to become the undisputed world middleweight champion.

CIRCUS

Robert Klein

Memories of "The Greatest Show on Earth®"

Spring, and respite from cold weather in the Bronx of my childhood in the fifties had several unmistakable signs. We took out our baseball gloves to "have a catch." We shed our cumbersome winter coats. But the most ubiquitous portent of the warming season was the sight of the poster of a growling tiger, in every merchant's store, announcing that the Ringling Bros. and Barnum & Bailey® circus would be making its annual sojourn to Madison Square Garden.

Any parent with a heart could not deny their progeny the thrill of seeing The Greatest Show on Earth®, the famously immodest slogan of the production. Actually, in a technical sense, to me, Cynthia Bernstein, my neighbor getting ready for bed in the window across the street, was the greatest show on earth, but that's another story. The circus, with its tigers jumping through flaming hoops, seven-foot brown bears dancing with blondes, and Unis, who could balance on his index finger on a lit globe, was irresistible.

My mother would take my sister Rhoda, me, and a couple of cousins, on the D train to the old Garden on Eighth Avenue and Fiftieth Street. The first ritual was buying a hot dog and an orange drink from the Nedick's stand in front of the building. Then, we walked toward the entrance, with hawkers of souvenirs and programs shouting, "Who needs a program? Program here!" Suddenly, there it was, the mysterious sideshow. There was the tallest man, the fattest lady, the world's largest frame, the smallest physique, and other terrible misfortunes of nature that adhered to the mind and imagination of a little boy.

Above all, wafting slowly at first, and then in a torrent, until the overwhelming sensation could not go unnoticed: the smell of elephants. This was a rather exotic odor for Eighth Avenue and Fiftieth Street, but it was a part of the excitement and the mystery of the circus. If truth be told, I didn't mind that smell at all.

As the lights dimmed in the giant Garden, the children spun their luminous sticks, making for a surreal and thrilling sight of multicolor motion, prefiguring the psychedelic screen savers, which would not arrive until thirty years later.

Though I begged my mom for a souvenir circus whip, she refused to buy me one. She was certain that I would poke someone's eye out, or possibly take out my own with it. I had to settle for a balloon, which, I might point out, was attached to a stick, which could easily have taken my eye out.

Then there was Emmett Kelly, the great unsmiling clown, who would sweep up the spotlight on the ground patiently, only to have it spread out all over the floor again. When I go to see my Knicks in the present-day Garden when the circus is in town, the perfume of the pachyderms sends me back to those days of wonder. And I wonder all over again how all those clowns could fit in that tiny car.

PREVIOUS SPREAD
Ringling Bros. and Barnum & Bailey® circus elephants have been performing at the Garden for its entire history. The legendary Jumbo debuted at the Garden in 1882 and was the pet of P.T. Barnum.

OPPOSITE
1972 - Otto Griebling, one of the greatest circus clowns ever, after a performance. Griebling passed away from throat cancer in his dressing room shortly after this photo was taken.

Emmett Kelly was everybody's favorite clown.
He entertained circus audiences for over five
decades as "Weary Willie," and performed on
Broadway, in television, and in the movies as well.

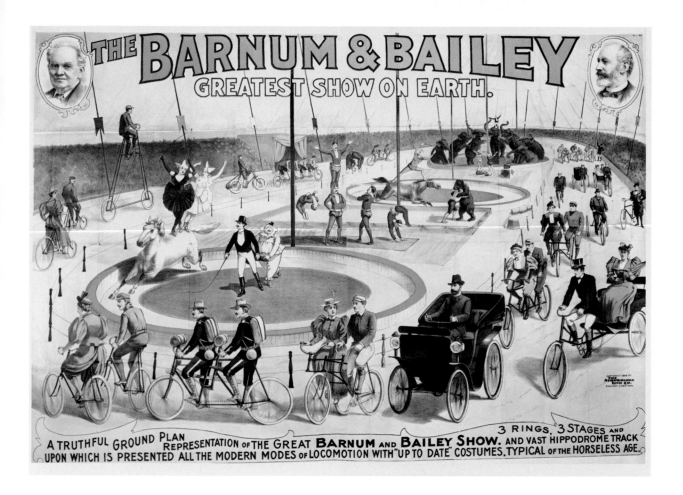

TOP
1896 – It was Barnum who coined the phrase
"The Greatest Show On Earth®," and the return
of the three rings to the Garden every year
continues to be one of the surest signs of spring.

BOTTOM
Gunther Gebel-Williams, universally known as
the greatest animal trainer of all time, performed
in The Greatest Show On Earth® for more than
a quarter of a century.

Never missing a show during his entire American performing career — a run of more than 12,000 performances — Gunther Gebel-Williams was inducted into the Madison Square Garden Walk of Fame in 1995.

Everyone loves a clown — the colorful face of one of the many Ringling Bros. and Barnum & Bailey® clowns.

ABOVE
Horses were the first animal circus performers, and are still big "stars" today. Their performances are loved by children of all ages.

Spike Lee

The Fan Who Got Into the Game

I was eight years old when I started attending basketball games at the old Garden with my dad, and we sat upstairs in the nose-bleed seats. That's all we could afford and that was fine with us.

Sitting up in those seats, I marveled at Clyde. He was amazing! He was the quintessential defensive player, and was so smooth he could steal the ball from another player without the player ever knowing it.

It was in those seats on May 8, 1970, where I watched Willis Reed limp onto the court in the seventh game of the 1970 NBA championship series. I will always remember that magic moment and the electricity in the Garden.

As my life progressed from film school to making commercials and movies, I bought progressively better Knicks seats as well, eventually ending up with courtside seats. It's a whole different world sitting courtside. I'm part of the game — just ask Reggie Miller.

"At Patrick Ewing night, the fans showed their great appreciation and love for the many wonderful memories that he had given them."

One of my greatest moments at the Garden was attending Patrick Ewing Night on February 28, 2003. I first watched Patrick play in the Big East Tournament against St. John's when he and coach John Thompson of Georgetown University were the enemy. The crowd was rooting for the local St. John's team, and their two star players, Chris Mullin and Mark Jackson. Those Georgetown versus St. John's games were some of the greatest basketball games I've ever seen at the Garden. You could see Patrick was going to be great. I was a Hoya supporter.

The night they retired Patrick's number was a night that stood out in Knicks' history. The fans showed their great appreciation and love for the many wonderful years and memories that Patrick had given them. NBA greats including Michael Jordan, Charles Barkley, Julius (Dr. J) Erving, Clyde Drexler, Willis Reed, Walt Frazier, John Starks, Bernard King, and Alonzo Mourning all came out to honor Patrick. The ceremonies started with the entire current Knicks team wearing #33 jerseys. Allan Houston presented Patrick with the keys to a Hummer and his former teammates presented him with a bronze statue showing Patrick with his arms up celebrating the moment the Knicks won the 1994 Eastern Conference championship. Willis Reed presented him with a photo-montage that spanned his career both on and off the court and Patrick's former opponents gave him a rack of #33 jerseys from the greatest players in all sports who ever wore #33. To have his banner raised to the Garden rafters alongside those of Willis Reed, Walt Frazier, Bill Bradley, Dave DeBusschere, Earl Monroe, Dick Barnett, Dick McGuire, and Red Holzman was a well-deserved honor.

PREVIOUS SPREAD
June 5, 1994 – With a Game Seven win over Indiana
in the Eastern Conference Finals, the Knickerbockers
advanced to their first NBA Finals in twenty-one years.

ABOVE
February 28, 2003 – On Patrick Ewing Night,
#33 took his final curtain call.

The big emotional moment came when Patrick spoke and was so eloquent in front of 20,000 cheering fans. The outpouring of affection that Patrick and the fans had for each other was expressed when he said "I will always be a New Yorker." The fans recognized and appreciated all that Patrick had brought to the Knicks for the fifteen years he poured his heart and soul onto the court. No Knicks fan will ever forget what Patrick brought to the franchise — for fifteen years, a franchise-record 1,174 games, there was never a moment that he didn't give over 100% — he came to play. The evening was a fitting tribute to recognize the career of one of the greatest Knicks ever.

I'm thrilled to be able to watch a great Garden moment from the best seat in the house, but will never forget watching Clyde, Willis, Barnett, Dollar Bill, DeBusschere, Earl the Pearl, Phil Jackson, Cazzie Russell, Dan Stallworth, and coach Red Holzman from the blue seats.

ABOVE
The original 1946-47 Knicks during training camp at Bear Mountain, New York.

"I remember that when you bounced the ball, it wouldn't come up from the dead wood of the floor, and when you shot a free throw, some guys would be jiggling the hanging wire. But it was a thrill to play there."

– OSCAR ROBERTSON

TOP
Hall of Fame coach Joe Lapchick piloted the Knicks to three straight East crowns in the early 1950s, with the likes of (L to R) Harry Gallatin, Dick McGuire, and Carl Braun.

BOTTOM
In 1950, Coach Lapchick welcomed the Knicks' first African-American player, former Globetrotter Nat "Sweetwater" Clifton.

"Basketball is a city game
and Madison Square Garden
is the Mecca."

– WALT FRAZIER

May 4, 1970 – The Captain – Willis Reed – crashed
to the floor during the opening minutes of Game Five
of the NBA Finals.

Ed Bradley

Willis Leads the Way

In 1969, I was working at WCBS Newsradio as a reporter covering general news in New York City. I convinced the station that the Knicks were a good story for us to cover and that they had a chance to make the playoffs. I sat at a courtside table filing live reports after every quarter and interviewing players after the game. They made the playoffs that year but were eliminated. By the following season, they were not only ready for the playoffs but with an eighteen-game winning streak were a legitimate contender for the championship.

The players were a team in the classic sense of the word: *a group organized to work together*. There were those players who stood out more than others but on any night anyone on the starting five could rise above the others and be the person who led the team that night. It all started with coach Red Holzman and his philosophy of defense first. It was their belief in his system that brought the Knicks the first championship in their history.

And what a group of players! Willis Reed was the captain and foundation of the team. He could score inside and out, he could rebound and he proved throughout the season that he could play hurt with the heart of a champion. Walt Frazier was the kind of ball handling guard who could do whatever the team needed — score, distribute the ball, shut down his man on defense or make a key steal. Dave DeBusschere was a horse on the boards and a tough defender who could also score. Dollar Bill, Bill Bradley, was also called Mr. President by some teammates. He seemed to never stop running, had a deadly jump shot and could pass like a guard. Dick Barnett was as smart and as tough as they come and had a shot from the corner that was strange and unorthodox but deadly accurate. Cazzie Russell, who could have started for most teams in the league, was a scoring machine off the bench and was the player who introduced the team to health food. When he was hot, he couldn't be stopped. Mike Riordan, Phil Jackson, and Dave Stallworth were ultimate role players providing critical minutes and at times inspirational play.

In the championship Finals, Willis went down with a painful hip injury in Game Five and so did the hopes of the fans who longed for that first championship. He didn't play in the sixth game and wasn't on the court for warm-ups of the deciding seventh game. Without the captain, the Wilt Chamberlain-led Lakers with Jerry West and Elgin Baylor had to be big favorites. Then a jolt of electricity shot through the Garden. Willis walked onto the floor dressed to play. There was hope! Still limping and barely able to get up and down the court, he nailed his first two shots and the Knicks were off and running. For all practical purposes the game was over. Willis didn't play much that night but the *team* picked him up; Frazier scored 36 points and handed out an incredible 19 assists. When the game was over, the players poured on to the floor, swept up in the emotion of actually winning a championship and basking in the waves of emotion from more than 19,000 fans.

In the locker room after the game, the interviews were almost giddy and there was as much beer as champagne, which was mostly poured or sprayed on each other and anyone who happened to be there. The joy in the Garden was a tonic to the city; New York finally had a championship team! It had been a magical season and I had the privilege of watching it from the best seat I would ever have in the Garden.

OPPOSITE
May 8, 1970 – "The Captain Returns." Willis Reed's
walk to glory.

ABOVE
Earl Monroe vs. Walt Frazier, 1970 Playoffs.

TOP
May 8, 1970 – After twenty-four years, the Knicks were champions. Bill Bradley, Nate Bowman, and Dave DeBusschere provide a champagne shower for ABC's Howard Cosell.

BOTTOM
May 10, 1973 – Three years later, at Los Angeles, the Knicks nailed down their second NBA crown. Jerry Lucas, Walt Frazier, Willis Reed, Phil Jackson, and Bill Bradley flashed a winner's salute.

LEFT
The quintessential Clyde.

RIGHT
Willis Reed vs. Boston's Dave Cowens,
1973 Playoffs.

Woody Allen

A Confessional

Here's the awful truth: although I am a great Knicks fan, I am not a good Knicks fan. True, I love the Knicks dearly and have spent, through the years, many a fourth quarter nervous over every possession or missed foul shot, but I definitely lack the winning-is-all-that-matters personality of the truly orthodox.

My allegiance, I must admit, is to exciting basketball. It is not simply for the Knicks to wind up with a W if it means I have to sit through a boring blowout. I don't have any fun at all when there's five minutes left and our boys are crushing their opponent by 20 points. I root for the opponent to catch up and pass the Knicks. Then I like the Knicks to overtake them; this makes the victory all the more fun. The problem is that even if the Knicks don't overtake them and finally lose the game, I feel I've had a more exciting evening.

> "I don't have any fun at all when there's five minutes left and our boys are crushing their opponent by 20 points. I root for the opponent to catch up and pass the Knicks."

Also, I have too much of a weakness for drama and aesthetics to be very chauvinistic. Theater is more important to me than the outcome. For example, I don't think I've ever pulled for Michael Jordan to miss one of his lovely, theatrical shots against anyone, including the Knickerbockers. Nor did I fail to body-English every basket Earl Monroe attempted as he dazzled everyone at Madison Square Garden when he was a Baltimore Bullet. It didn't matter if Earl's shot was the game winner; if "The Pearl," with all his star charisma, threw it up, I prayed it went in. To further inflame the faithful, I must also add that few players have given me more pleasure to watch than Reggie Miller, and seeing him beat the New York team in the final seconds, as is his dramatic habit, has its own special show-business beauty.

This shameful disloyalty even held true when I rooted for the greatest team the Knicks ever put on the floor and one of the greatest in all the annals of the sport. The championship Knicks of 1973 were just such a perfect blend of art and science that they fulfilled every desire the most picayune fan could have. I don't ever remember experiencing any problem with their march to the title — except — well, I'll come to it. For one thing, they were the most beautifully-knit unit I'd ever seen on a court. Willis Reed was the centerpiece and simply was a winner. He carried himself like a winner, played like a winner, and his mere presence in the lineup affected the confidence and well-being of the entire team.

The two forwards, Dave DeBusschere and Bill Bradley, were huge basketball talents. DeBusschere was a master of defense, could rebound fiercely and shoot effectively from long distance. Bradley passed the ball with confident brilliance and was perfectly capable of scoring 30-plus points if the occasion so demanded. The three frontliners were all highly intelligent, very poised, and could bring the team back from a large deficit to win. (Large deficits for the Knicks were rare things in those days, but when they occurred, they proved no problem.)

Walt Frazier, of course, was in a class by himself. I think he was, pound for pound, the greatest Knick of all time and that includes Patrick Ewing, his only real competition for that honor. Frazier was actually then among the three best guards who had ever suited up to play the sport and in his era ranked right alongside Oscar Robertson and Jerry West, the two other titans. He was flawless in all aspects of basketball and when it was necessary to steal the ball away from an opponent, he did just that. He was great to look at (good casting) — handsome, tall but not outsized, remarkably erect posture (even to this day), with absolute control of the ball. As for scoring, he piled up the points season after season with a picture-perfect jump shot. He was said by other athletes to be the best-coordinated athlete of any athlete playing in any sport at the time. The fifth man was the Knicks' old nemesis, Earl Monroe, who came over from Baltimore and completed the final piece of this superb mosaic.

Every New York fan remembers when the news came that we had acquired "The Pearl." All the crepehangers immediately said the dazzling guard was too great a soloist to fit in with such a well-structured team; that he and Frazier couldn't possibly play together. Of course, in short order they became the greatest guard tandem of all time, won the championship, and both went on to the Hall of Fame, that pantheon with the silly name.

Despite their success, I was likely the only Knicks fan who looked upon that fabulous year bittersweetly, and here is my cavil. I, amongst all my friends, couldn't help wondering if Earl Monroe's great sacrifice, the voluntary reigning in of his flamboyant theatrical court genius to become a cog in an organized unit wasn't too high a price to pay for a ring. In my heart, to see him perform at Madison Square Garden with the unequalled creativity he glowed with as a Baltimore Bullet, would have been more captivating to behold than his integration into a well-oiled machine, albeit a championship one. That's why I say that, while I may be a great Knicks fan, I'm not what you'd call a good one. I have too many weaknesses.

ABOVE

November 18, 1972 – Just one game, one early-season Saturday night, yet it defined a team and an era. With 19 straight points over the game's final 5:11, the Knicks authored their greatest regular-season comeback, defeating the Milwaukee Bucks 87-86, surviving a last-second shot by Kareem Adbul-Jabbar #33, and sending the Garden into a frenzy at the final buzzer.

LEFT
The unstoppable Bernard King lit up the Garden in the mid-1980s.

RIGHT
May 25, 1993 – John Starks flew over a trio of Chicago Bulls (Horace Grant, Bill Cartwright, and Michael Jordan) for "The Dunk," sealing the Knicks' triumph in Game Two of the Eastern Conference Finals.

LEFT
One of the signature figures of "the city game," the electrifying Stephon Marbury returned to his hometown as a Knick in 2003-04.

RIGHT
Allan Houston has written his name among the team's greatest.

Matthew Modine

The World's Most Famous Arena

Sometimes titles are given. Sometimes they are handed down, passed from generation to generation. But more often than not, especially in New York City, titles can only be earned. Time erodes memory and what remains, what endures and weathers the seasons of change, is hard, unarguable truth and extraordinary accomplishment. Great battles. Amazing performances. Events that become defining moments in our lives. Phenomena that give context to eras. Being witness to human brilliance. Madison Square Garden did not inherit its title. The title wasn't handed down. It has earned the right to proudly call itself "The World's Most Famous Arena."

I've been to other arenas around the country: the old Salt Palace in Salt Lake City, the Forum in Los Angeles, the San Diego Sports Arena, Market Square Arena in Indianapolis, and the old Chicago Stadium. I've seen great events and had great times in all those buildings. But none of the venues have the audacity to call themselves "The World's Most Famous Arena." But then, none of the other arenas have made the hair on the back of my neck stand up or made my heart beat a bit faster just by walking into the building. I start to feel it when I get within a couple blocks of the Garden. Maybe it's the millions of commuters that pass beneath each day in the cavernous Penn Station. Or perhaps it's because the Garden sits in the heart of the most exciting city in the world.

"But then, none of the other arenas have made the hair on the back of my neck stand up or made my heart beat a bit faster just by walking into the building."

For me, it's the Knicks. Win or lose, I love the Knicks. It was my future wife Cari (a wonderful and committable Knicks fan!) who first brought me to see a Knicks game. For some reason, it was like the first basketball game I'd ever seen. It was just different. You hear and read about the fans at the Garden and it's true. They understand the game. They know the players and the rules better than any place I've watched a game. Then there are the New York Liberty fans. Going to see the Liberty games is a whole other deal. Loud? You don't know loud, screaming, hysterical passion until you witness the ladies in action.

Sitting with my wife at games over the past two decades is an education in what it means to love your home team, to be passionate about athletic prowess. What I like most about the fans in New York is their appreciation for commitment and hard work. They'll forgive a bad night, but won't tolerate inconsistency and lack of effort. Great qualities to strive for in all walks of life. I'm sure there are similar wonderful moments happening in arenas all over the world, but I'm positive none so often as at "The World's Most Famous Arena!"

OPPOSITE
Clash of the Titans — Ewing vs. Jordan,
1989 Playoffs.

ABOVE

June 5, 1999 – Amid a scene of Garden hysteria, Larry Johnson (#2) headed upcourt after nailing a 3-point bomb in the waning moments of Game Three of the Eastern Conference Finals against Indiana. LJ's free throw completed his unforgettable four-point play and gave the Knicks a vital win in their improbable march to the NBA Finals.

LIBERTY

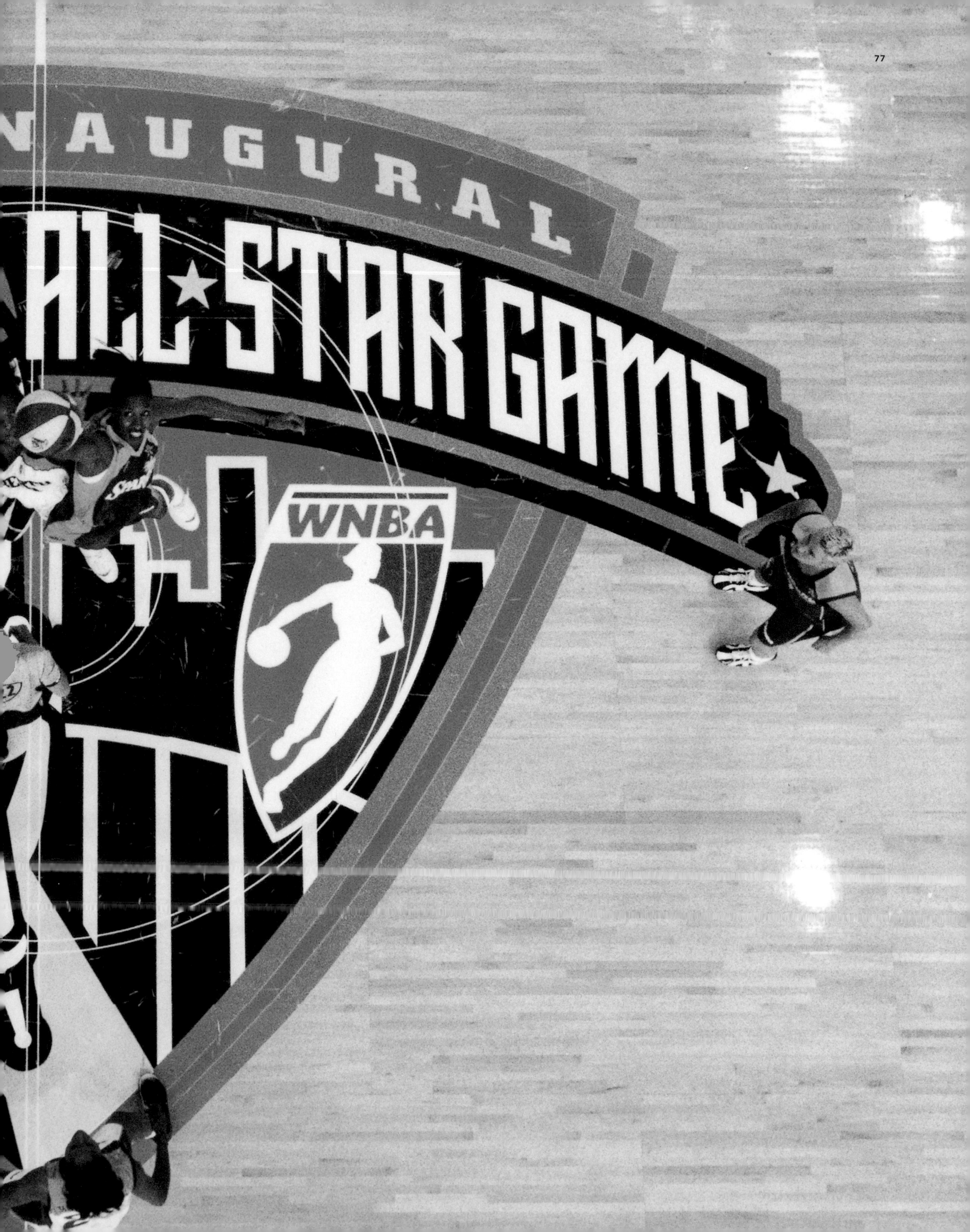
NAUGURAL
ALL STAR GAME
WNBA

Joan Jett

Liberty for All

I bought myself Liberty season tickets with great excitement.

I'd done a recording of the theme song to the *Mary Tyler Moore* television show, and it had been adopted as an unofficial anthem of women's college basketball. Because of that, I'd been invited to attend some college games. For a sports fan like myself, it was thrilling to see the beauty and intensity at which the game was being played on the college level. These girls were taking the game seriously. It seemed we had our farm teams...could the dream of professional women's basketball be far behind?

The atmosphere at the Garden was immediately different for the Liberty. People of all ages were there, fathers bringing their daughters, mothers bringing their sons. Teenagers. Celebrities. Everyone had a good time and wanted this team, and the league, to succeed. The Garden and the Liberty began what would become their own traditions, and no one needed any coaxing to join in. It was innocent and joyful.

Because of the efforts I've made in my own career to achieve longevity and a level of excellence, I appreciate the effort these women have made since girlhood to master a sport to a professional status. They are pioneers and trailblazers, not only in women's sports but also in lifting the spirits and expectations of women. They deserve much respect.

"Sometimes, when good things happen, I tell myself that I helped. Isn't that part of the magic of being a sports fan?"

There is no place like Madison Square Garden. It is the ultimate rock concert venue, the Mecca of boxing, and a shrine to the Knicks and the Rangers. The Garden holds the same allure to WNBA players as to members of other sports teams. Coming to New York is exciting, playing in the Garden makes you part of the long hallowed history of professional sports. There is a sense among us all at the games, that the Liberty fit right into the Garden's standard of professionalism, and that greatness is within our reach.

Being a season ticket holder is something I do for myself. I'm an emotional fan. I'm loud. I cheer. I try to psych out the other team, whether it's bringing in a voodoo doll or screaming "Defense!" to encourage my side and unnerve the other.

Sometimes, when good things happen, I tell myself that I helped. Isn't that part of the magic of being a sports fan? The belief that wishing makes it so? And so I bring all that to the games, making each one a special and satisfying experience.

But in the end it's about the game. I find the Liberty particularly interesting to watch because they've evolved a unique style of play reminiscent of the sport my Dad watched when he was a kid, before there

OPPOSITE RIGHT
August 24, 2002 – Joan Jett hexes the opposition.

were so many giants. It's not an above-the-rim game, like the men play. In the women's game, the players depend even more on ball movement.

I've had a lot of young girls tell me they felt okay about learning to play electric guitar because I helped make it seem a normal, natural thing. So when I see all the young girls watching these great women athletes, I feel uplifted, knowing that the old stereotypes are fading and a new generation of women will go into professional team sports with much more confidence and no inhibitions.

The fans are all enjoying these halcyon days. In twenty years, our game may be taller, faster, and rougher, but we'll all remember how we were part of a societal revolution — the beginning of women's professional team sports — and the Garden was our sandbox.

LEFT
July 12, 2003 – The WNBA All-Star Game returned to the Garden as Tari Phillips jumped against Lisa Leslie.

TOP
August 25, 2002 – The franchise's emotional leader, Teresa Weatherspoon, led the Liberty to four WNBA Finals.

ABOVE
June 22, 2003 – Becky Hammon rises to the hoop.

COLLEGE BASKETBALL

Bill Bradley
From the Court to the Rostrum

Many memorable moments in my life took place in Madison Square Garden. In the late 1960s, the building became my home as a member of a New York Knicks team that won two NBA Championships. Later, I would revisit the Garden as both politician and fan. But on December 30, 1964, I was just twenty-one years old and had only one thing on my mind: beating Michigan.

It was the semifinal round of the ECAC Holiday Festival, and no one gave our Princeton team much of a chance against the number-one team in the nation, the University of Michigan. All-American Cazzie Russell, a future teammate of mine on the Knicks, was Michigan's star player, and I was Princeton's go-to forward.

More than 18,500 people, a standing-room-only crowd, attended the game at the Old Garden on Eighth Avenue. Yet, in the years since, it seems as if at least 21,475 people have stopped me to say that they saw the game and will never forget it.

"Something about that game made a very strong impression on people. No one expected it to be that close."

Princeton led by as many as 14 points in the second half. But with about three minutes to go, I fouled out of the game. Quickly, our double-digit lead dwindled. You can imagine how frustrated I felt, after scoring 41 points, to sit on that bench and watch the lead dissipate. Michigan closed the game with a 17-1 run, with Russell scoring 9 of their 17 points, securing the Wolverines' 80-78 victory.

I also remember the irrepressible New York sportswriters that night. I recall being interviewed by the thoughtful Leonard Koppett of the *Times*, the fiery Dick Young of the *Daily News* and Milton Gross, Lenny Lewin, and Leonard Schecter of the *Post*. They made that night a part of Garden folklore just as a few years later, they made our championship Knicks teams synonymous with teamwork.

Why were those Knicks championship teams so memorable? I think it was because we meshed as players and as human beings. We brought out the best in each other. We were like a five-pointed star, and each of us realized that no one of us could be as good individually as we all were together. We sent people a message about unity and teamwork that transcended basketball and for a time captured the imagination of New York.

As players, we realized that the fans at the Garden were the most knowledgeable fans in the country. We played the game the way New Yorkers liked it: gritty, but full of finesse. They would applaud the pass that led to the pass that set up the basket, something that didn't happen at most arenas. I remember a play with Walt Frazier in which he would go backdoor and I'd hit him with a pass for a basket. I always felt the fans applauded for Frazier's scoring *and* my assist.

PREVIOUS SPREAD
College basketball's Mecca, Garden III, during the late-1960s.

ABOVE
December 30, 1964 – ECAC Holiday Festival,
Russell vs. Bradley.

"I was at the (Bill) Bradley-(Cazzie) Russell game screaming my head off. The fact that I had the opportunity to come back and play in this building as a collegian meant a lot to my career and my life."

– KAREEM ABDUL-JABBAR

LEFT
January 9, 1958 – Oscar Robertson poured in a Garden III record 56 points against Seton Hall.

RIGHT
March 1950 – Coach Nat Holman reached for the sky after his City College Beavers captured both the NCAA and NIT titles, a golden moment for CCNY.

For all of us, our crowning moment came on May 8, 1970, in the seventh game of the NBA Finals against the Los Angeles Lakers. Willis Reed, our captain and leader, had been injured in the fifth game, and nobody knew if he was going to play in the deciding contest. But when he limped onto the court, the Garden erupted. I saw Wilt Chamberlain, Elgin Baylor, and Jerry West turn and look at Willis as if to say, "This guy is going to play?!" On one of the first plays, Willis got the ball about seventeen feet from the basket, shot and scored. A few plays later he hit a second basket. The crowd was so loud that I thought the roof would blow off.

Willis's dramatic entrance catapulted us forward. Walt Frazier had an incredible game, the rest of us played very well, and we won our first championship. Willis's effort was a metaphor for the fact that the whole team refused to quit. With five seconds left on the clock, I started to celebrate, somewhat prematurely. Garden photographer George Kalinsky caught me with both of my fists in the air in what was an expression of pure joy that was shared by all Knicks fans.

After my playing career ended, I entered the world of politics. People have often asked me what was the biggest thrill — winning the two NBA championships or the three terms in the U.S. Senate. I consider being elected to the U.S. Senate three times by the people of New Jersey as the biggest honor in my life. But, the day after being elected I realized that for the next six years I had to work to make sure I proved the voters right. But as for my biggest thrill in life, along with the birth of our daughter, it was unquestionably winning two championships for the Knicks in 1970 and 1973. On the court, standing, with fists raised in the air, chills coursing up my spine, and a smile that was so wide it ached, I realized that we were the best in the world.

I've had other memorable evenings at the Garden. I attended the 1980 and 1992 Democratic conventions. In 1980, I listened as Jimmy Carter was nominated. In 1992, I made one of the keynote speeches, while the video board behind me showed my retired #24 that was hanging from the rafters.

On November 17, 1999, when I was running for the presidency, I had a major fund-raising event at the Garden. It included fifteen all-time NBA greats. Some were my former teammates and some were former opponents. Each was a friend who came to offer support of my candidacy by giving testimony to the bond formed during our years together in the sport.

ABOVE
Before dominating the NBA as Kareem Abdul-Jabbar,
Lew Alcindor returned to his hometown and won MVP
honors at the 1968 Holiday Festival.

I recognize that players and performers draw the crowds, but there are also unsung heroes who make the Garden work. I think of the guys who lay down the basketball court over the ice rink and take it back up again. I think of the ticket takers, the security guards, the vendors and the people behind the scenes who meant so much to me, like John Condon, Dr. Yanagisawa, Danny Whelan, and Feets Broudy. Each of these individuals, and so many more, played a role in making the Garden come alive for me.

I've celebrated four life milestones at the Garden: bursting on the college scene in New York, winning two championships with the Knicks, participating in the presidential conventions, and having a unique presidential fund-raiser. My only regret is never having been a clown in the circus. If I could be a clown in the circus — just once — that would complete my Garden journey.

"This arena is the greatest in the world.
It's in the greatest city in the world. And
it has the greatest fans in the world."

– LOU CARNESECCA

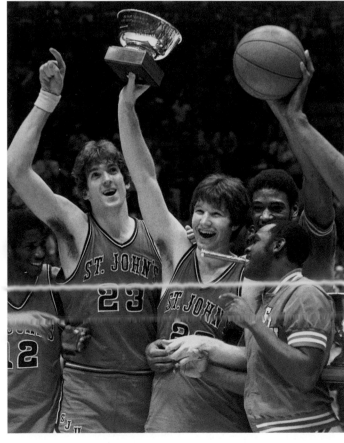

LEFT
March 1983 – St. John's — led by All-American
Chris Mullin (center) — celebrated its first Big East title.

RIGHT
March 6, 1977 – Montclair State's Carol Blazejowski
poured in 52 points against Queens College, still the
Garden IV single-game college point scoring record.

SPECIAL EVENTS

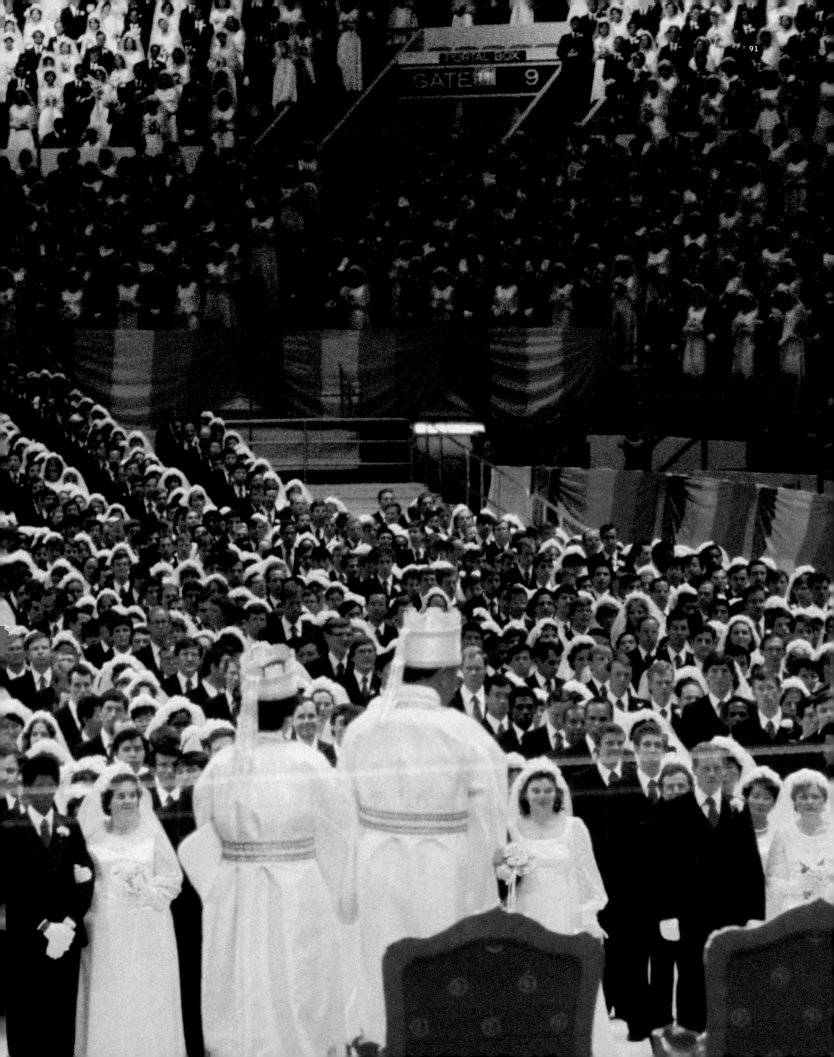

Barbara Eden

A Night for the Stars

Photographers' bulbs were flashing, and limousines were double-parked on Seventh Avenue. Opening night at the new Madison Square Garden, February 11, 1968, was a salute to the United Service Organization (USO). The show starred Bob Hope and Bing Crosby, and I had the pleasure of joining them on the bill, that snowy night in New York.

I remember the hoopla, the glamour, and the anticipation of breaking in a new arena. Bing's beautiful wife was there as well, wearing a miniskirt despite the weather. But when I reflect on opening night, it was the teamwork between two classic performers that really stands out. I'm referring to the teamwork of Bob Hope and Bing Crosby.

In one sketch, Bob got into the ring and "fought" the champion of the world, Rocky Marciano. Bing played his manager and I was Bob's nurse, all dressed in white, ready to administer first aid if he got knocked out. And, since we were playing it for laughs, Bob got knocked off his feet like a punching bag. Of course, Bob knew how to take a pratfall.

But he was beginning to have problems with his eyesight about that time and was having difficulty reading the cue cards while he was in the ring. Bing, his longtime partner, sensed what was going on and stepped in to help him. He leaped into the ring, approached Bob, and started whispering his lines into his ear. Bing was so subtle that the audience could barely see his lips moving; it appeared as if the manager was giving his fighter some advice. Since I was so close to them, I was probably the only person there who knew what was happening.

I also recall having my own difficulties during that performance. In one scene, I was walking a huge St. Bernard on a short leash. The dog was nearly uncontrollable and started dragging me around onstage. The scene was rehearsed so often that the rough edges of the leash cut into my hands: I looked down and actually saw blood on them.

Ironically, a representative from the American Society for the Prevention of Cruelty to Animals was in rehearsal and complained to the producer about the dog being dragged on stage. What about the performer, I thought to myself?

Another number incorporated a group of chorus boys. The riser on the stage was really high, and Miriam Nelson, the choreographer, had staged a finale that had me perched atop a spectacular human pyramid, being caught by the boys as I fell backward. That was a bit scary, but it worked out just fine.

While many people remember me from *I Dream of Jeannie*, I actually performed in twenty-one network television Bob Hope specials. I felt great admiration for both Bob and Bing that night and for their obvious mutual affection. Being onstage with them brought back a rush of memories of seeing them on the big screen when I was growing up in San Francisco. Looking back, I feel lucky to have marked the opening of the new Madison Square Garden with these two legends of show business.

ABOVE
October 17, 1957 – Mike Todd threw a party marking the
one-year anniversary of the release of his movie *Around the
World in 80 Days*. 18,000 people were invited, and his wife
Elizabeth Taylor hosted.

"I can now retire from politics after having had 'Happy Birthday' sung to me in such a sweet, wholesome way."

— PRESIDENT JOHN F. KENNEDY

ABOVE

May 19, 1962 – Approximately 17,000 people attended the Democratic Party fund-raiser and birthday salute for President John F. Kennedy. It featured a host of stars, including Marilyn Monroe, who sang a breathy night-club version of "Happy Birthday" to the President.

George Kalinsky

His Holiness Visits the Garden

The Pope's visit to Madison Square Garden, on October 3, 1979, taught me something about the meaning of spirituality. John Paul II had recently been elected Pope, and this journey to the United States marked his first official visit as spiritual leader of the Roman Catholic Church. His appearance at Madison Square Garden was the centerpiece of his tour.

I was waiting for him backstage with a host of Garden officials. When his limousine arrived, Cardinal John O'Connor got out from the front seat and asked me to open the door for the Pope. As His Holiness arose out of the back seat, I first saw his white robe, which emitted a brilliant light. The moment was ineffable, powerful, and spiritual.

> "I first saw his white robe, which emitted a brilliant light. The moment was ineffable, powerful, and spiritual."

For a moment, I was unable to take photographs. I gazed at the Pope's eyes, which were comforting, warm, and kind. He eased out of the limousine and I mustered up the courage to say, "Welcome to Madison Square Garden." Minutes later, the pontiff entered the arena, which was filled to capacity with more than 20,000 people. He was greeted by the strains of the "William Tell" Overture. The assembled crowd, many of whom were children and young adults, roared their approval. When the Pope spotted six-year-old Geralyn Smith sitting in the front row, he beckoned her forward. He swept the shy little girl into his arms and hoisted her atop the "Popemobile" for the whole world to see. As he smiled at her, to the delight of the crowd, I was able to capture that great moment on film.

That photo captured the spiritual impact that the Pope could have on one person and, at the same time, on millions of people.

OPPOSITE
October 3, 1979 – In a touching moment, Pope John Paul II lifted Geralyn Smith up from the crowd during his Garden visit for the world to see.

Billy Crystal   **Athlete of the Century**

As a sports fan who grew up in New York, I've been in Madison Square Garden for some unforgettable occasions. I used to go to Holiday Festivals with my dad in the old Garden feeling the crowd love the great St. John's teams. I was at the Garden when Wilt Chamberlain scored 71 points with a broken nose, and I remember Dave DeBusschere scoring 39 against Philadelphia on my birthday one year. I saw many great Knicks games with Patrick Ewing, including the trip to the Finals in 1994. But being asked to present Muhammad Ali with the *Sports Illustrated* "Athlete of the Century" award in 1999, not 100 feet from where he and Joe Frazier had stood toe to toe in the "Fight of the Century," was significant for me.

Ali became a dear friend from our first meeting in 1975, when I imitated him for a *Sports Magazine* television special broadcast from the Plaza Hotel. My late friend Dick Schaap, who organized the show, helped us stay in touch and as the year passed, the three of us saw our paths become more and more intertwined. I know it sounds odd to say, "Here's my friend, Muhammad Ali," but that's what he's been to my family and me. When Lonnie Ali called to say, "It would mean a lot to Muhammad if you would present his award; we want you to do this," I was thrilled.

I had attended the Ali-Doug Jones fight in the old Garden back in 1963, and here I was, thirty-six years later, handing him this prestigious award. As he came toward me, he winked and threw some jabs at me; immediately a hush came over the crowd of over 10,000. The great man was going to speak.

Here was Muhammad Ali, the greatest athlete of our time, the one who spoke to our generation. Now tragically afflicted with Parkinson's disease, the crowd wondered if he was going to be able to say anything. I didn't know what he was going to do, and I was fully ready to hand him the award, stand back and wipe the tears from my eyes, and just watch people love him. That would have been plenty for me. But as the crowd stood and applauded, he handed me back the award, went to the podium, and made a short but eloquent speech.

It was astounding to see the assembled group of athletes who turned out to honor Muhammad. As I helped him off the stage, everybody in that audience just wanted to look at that great man. We took a group photo that included Jack Nicklaus, Arnold Palmer, Bill Russell, Kareem Abdul-Jabbar, Michael Jordan, Joe Montana, Chris Evert, Tiger Woods, and Wayne Gretzky, all the number-one athletes in their individual sports. Everyone wanted to take a picture with him. He'd put his hand up behind their heads, make rabbit ears, and then he'd wink, say something funny, and whisper something to them. They all wanted to shake Ali's hand or put their arm around him and, like little kids, have their picture taken with him.

It was truly an amazing moment. Muhammad could have asked anybody to give him this award, and the fact that he had thought of me made me feel incredibly fortunate to have ever known him and been touched by him.

OPPOSITE
December 2, 1999 – Muhammad Ali accepts his
Sports Illustrated "Athlete of the Century" Award.

Susan Lucci **Breaking My Losing Streak at the Garden**

It took the relocation of the Emmy Awards ceremony from Radio City Music Hall to the Theater at Madison Square Garden in May, 1999, to break my losing streak. Eighteen years in a row, I had been nominated for Lead Actress in a Daytime Drama Series for my performance as Erica Kane in *All My Children*. And every year a presenter read another actress's name as winner. As the cliché goes, I was always the bridesmaid but never the bride. I thought being nominated so many years in a row was a testament to my acting ability and popularity, but I was tired of reporters asking, "Do you think you'll ever win?"

In 1999, when Radio City Music Hall was under renovation, the ceremony was moved to the Garden. I had always loved going to the Garden to see the Knicks play, and I had seen Madonna in concert there, but frankly, after eighteen ceremonies, I didn't think that changing the venue would increase my chances of winning.

The night of the Emmys, my husband and I walked in on the red carpet, passing the many media members in attendance. Our seats were right next to Rosie O'Donnell's, and she leaned over and said, "Susan, when you go up tonight to accept the award, why don't you hand me your evening bag? Otherwise, when they say your name and you get overexcited, you'll step on it, and it won't be pretty." I looked at Rosie and replied, "That's sweet of you, but I'm probably not going up there."

I remember that actor Shamar Moore was presenting the award for Lead Actress. When he opened the envelope, he exclaimed, "The streak is over!" Frankly, since we were at the Garden, I thought he might be referring to some playoff game. It was May, playoff season. I didn't make the connection at all until Rosie reached over and grabbed my evening bag. Then my husband lifted me up by my elbow. I was so numb that I don't even remember hearing my name mentioned. In utter disbelief, I whispered in my husband's ear, "Are you sure?"

All those clichés about winners having their knees turn into Jell-O and barely being able to walk onto the stage are true. When I finally reached center stage and saw that the entire industry was on its feet, I felt honored. My husband tells me that the standing ovation lasted nine minutes. In the history of the universe, nine minutes may not seem like a long time, but for me, it was endless. Everyone in the audience who knew me was crying. I composed myself enough to thank the people who were instrumental in helping me get onto the podium.

Having lost eighteen times and won only once, I can tell you the difference. Winning is better! Not only was winning fun, but the attention after the award was exhilarating! I had agreed to do the cover of *People* magazine if I won, and they did a photo shoot with me the next morning. Mayor Rudy Giuliani presented me with a key to the city, and everywhere I went in New York, including the "21" Club for dinner and Serendipity with my daughter for ice cream, the waiters would sing or send champagne. When firemen in a New York City fire truck recognized me, they flashed me the thumbs-up sign. People still come up to me, five years later, and tell me they jumped up and down as they watched the ceremony at home on television when my name was announced.

For the rest of my life, when I think of Madison Square Garden, I'll always associate it with winning an Emmy award.

OPPOSITE
May 21, 1999 – "The streak is over!" The Emmy Award for Best Lead Actress in a Daytime Drama Series went to Susan Lucci.

TOP
March 14, 1972 – The 14th Annual Grammy Awards were held at the Garden. Ed Sullivan and Andy Williams were just a few of the stars who graced the stage that evening.

BELOW LEFT
Elmo and his Muppet friends in *Sesame Street Live* have entertained children at the Theater at Madison Square Garden for years.

BELOW RIGHT
December, 1998 – Theater-goers enjoyed a musical production of *A Christmas Carol* for ten holiday seasons at the Theater. Here, Roger Daltrey plays Scrooge.

LEFT
February 23, 2003 – The 45th Annual Grammy Awards featured the first time Simon & Garfunkel performed together in almost a decade.

TOP
February 23, 2003 – The 45th Annual Grammy Awards filled the Garden.

BOTTOM
February 23, 2003 – Gwen Stefani of No Doubt performs at the Grammy Awards. No Doubt won Best Pop Performance for "Underneath It All."

RANGERS

Marv Albert   **Once a Fan, Always a Fan**

When Ed Giacomin and Walt Frazier returned to the Garden after being traded from New York, it created two memorable nights for sports fans.

Giacomin, who from 1965-76 played his heart out night after night for the Rangers, was now facing them as an opponent. And Walt Frazier, who had helped the Knicks win two NBA championships, was returning to his former home court. The return of these two crowd favorites proved to be emotional for everyone.

When general manager Emile ("the Cat") Francis let stalwart goalie Ed Giacomin go to the Red Wings, it left many Rangers fans distraught. Despite the ups and downs of the Rangers in the 1960s and 1970s, the diminutive Giacomin gave 100% every game — darting for pucks, scrambling in front of the nets, exhorting his teammates. In fact, Giacomin was the Rangers' all-time leader in wins at 266 (since surpassed by Mike Richter's 301), and remains the shutout leader with 49.

> "When he returned to the Garden, they remembered how he had given his all,
> and they showed their appreciation and love for him."

As fate would have it, after the Red Wings acquired thirty-six-year-old Giacomin on waivers, on Halloween Day 1975, he would return to play at the Garden only three days later. Rangers coach Ron Stewart warned his team that the crowd would be cheering for Giacomin, against the home team.

When I entered the arena that night, I immediately saw the fans' response to the trade; hanging from the rafter was a banner that read, "The Cat Is a Rat." The minute Giacomin hit the ice in his red and white Red Wings uniform, the fans started cheering, "Eddie, Eddie, Eddie!" During the national anthem, the cheers intensified, becoming louder and louder. It was as if all the frustration the Rangers fans had felt over so many years was lifted by the return of their star goalie. Tears started streaming down Giacomin's face. He was crying uncontrollably, and the game hadn't even started.

Buoyed by the cheers of the Rangers fans, "Eddie" was energized to beat his former team. That night, Giacomin led Detroit to a 6-4 victory over the hometown Rangers. A local newspaper reported that after a goal scored by the Rangers, one of the players skated up to Giacomin and apologized for scoring it.

It's interesting to note that Eddie hadn't played well for the Rangers the previous year or two, and the fans had started to turn against him. But when he returned to the Garden, they remembered how he had given his all, and they showed their appreciation and love for him. Drained and exhausted afterward, Eddie told me that he'd never forget this game as long as he lived.

Nearly two years later, when Walt (Clyde) Frazier was traded from the Knicks to the Cleveland Cavaliers on October 7, 1977, he too returned to play against his former team, a mere ten days after being traded. Clyde was never one to show emotion when he played. Calm, even-keeled, and nonplussed were Clyde's

PREVIOUS SPREAD
Rangers coach Emile "the Cat" Francis behind
the Blueshirt bench in 1970.

ABOVE
November 2, 1975 – "Eddie! Eddie! Eddie!"

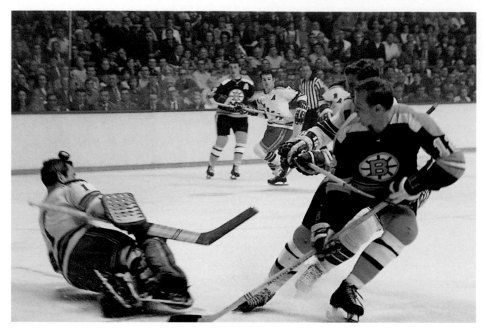

trademarks. Clearly now, however, he was bitter about being traded and wanted to show the Knicks management that they had made a mistake.

The Knicks fans, of course, knew what Frazier had meant to the Knicks. From 1967-1977, Frazier averaged 19.3 points per game, played in seven NBA All-Star games, and was named to seven NBA All-Defensive first teams. When center Willis Reed was injured in the 1970 NBA Finals, it was Clyde who scored 36 points and dished out 19 assists in Game Seven to pick up the team and lead them to victory.

Clyde told me before the game that he expected the crowd would boo him. But when public address announcer John Condon introduced him, instead the crowd erupted with cheers. They remembered how instrumental Clyde was in helping the Knicks win two championships, and they weren't going to let him forget it. Not only did the fans cheer, but every Knicks player rose from the bench and applauded Clyde.

Condon kept repeating, "Thank you, thank you," to the fans in an attempt to settle them down, but they just kept cheering. Clyde waved to the fans to calm them down; unlike Eddie Giacomin, he maintained his composure.

That night, Clyde scored 28 points and helped the Cavaliers beat the Knicks in overtime. The Knicks fans applauded every one of the points he scored.

When New York fans embrace players, they love them forever. Eddie's and Clyde's numbers were retired, and their jerseys now hang from the rafters in the Garden — two reminders of many memorable nights.

TOP
Giacomin vs. "The Big Bad Bruins."

TOP
The 1927-28 team, the first Rangers to win the Stanley Cup.

BELOW LEFT
Lester Patrick (L) and Garden mastermind Tex Rickard (R).

BELOW RIGHT
November 11, 1933 – NHL president Frank Calder honored 1933 Cup winners (L to R) Earl Seibert, Andy Aitkenhead, Ching Johnson, Frank Boucher, Bun Cook, and Bill Cook.

LEFT
December 3, 1947 – The House of Patrick:
Lester (C) with sons Muzz and Lynn on
Lester Patrick Night.

RIGHT
January 25, 1967 – On Harry Howell Night,
the legendary defenseman was honored as
the first player to appear in 1,000 games
as a Ranger.

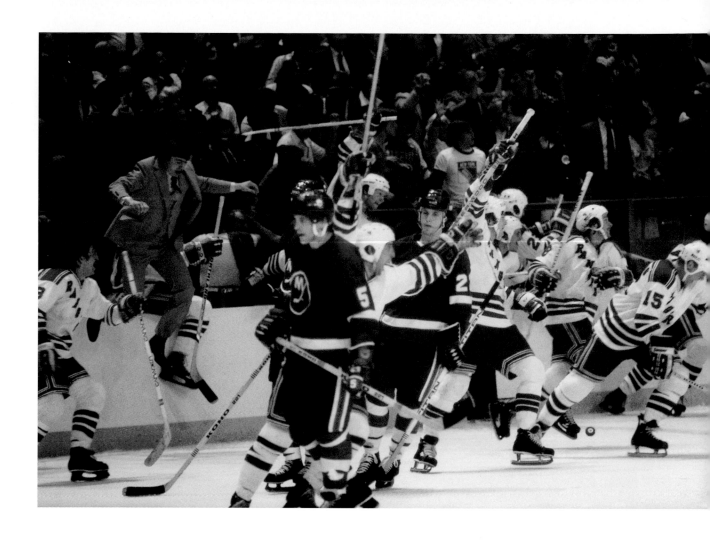

"From a player's perspective, Madison Square Garden is the greatest arena. There is a unique energy and electricity every time you're there."

– WAYNE GRETZKY

TOP
May 8, 1979 – The celebration began as the final buzzer sounded on the Rangers' stunning six-game triumph over the archrival Islanders in the Stanley Cup semifinals.

BOTTOM
Score!! Steve Vickers (foreground) lit the lamp against the Islanders in the 1979 Playoffs.

LEFT
January 22, 1994 – Brian Leetch, Mike Richter, Mark
Messier, and Adam Graves represented the Rangers at
the NHL All-Star Game at the Garden. Messier had a goal
and two assists, while Richter won game MVP honors.

RIGHT
June 14, 1994 – Mark Messier celebrated after scoring in
Game Seven of the Stanley Cup Finals. The goal put the
Rangers up 3-1 and turned out to be the game winner.

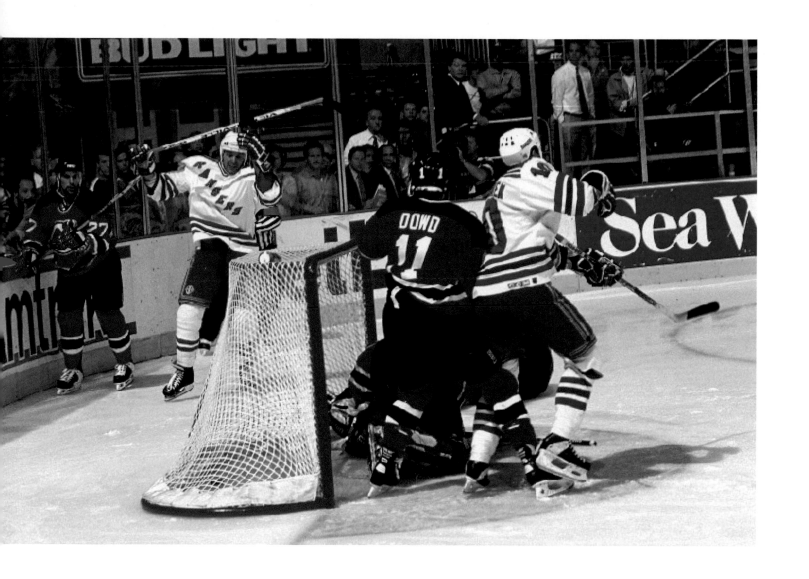

ABOVE
May 27, 1994 – "Matteau!! Matteau!! Matteau!!" Howie
Rose's radio call etched Stephane Matteau's goal into
memory. It gave the Blueshirts a 2-1 win over New Jersey
in Game Seven of the Eastern Conference Finals.

Tim Robbins

The Curse Is Lifted

I've spent many great nights in Madison Square Garden. As a child I cheered on the Rangers GAG line from the back row of the blue seats. I saw Bobby Orr kill a two minute penalty by himself without passing the puck. I was thrilled by Clyde Frazier and Willis Reed. And I saw Springsteen lift the roof in 1978. But the night that stands out far above the others was the night the curse was finally lifted, the night the Rangers won the Stanley Cup.

I was shooting a film during the '94 cup run and couldn't go to Game Five of the Finals, so I hired a satellite to get the game on location in rural New Jersey. Mercifully I had a few days off after that and took an early morning flight to Vancouver for Game Six. After suffering verbal abuse in Vancouver (for wearing my Rangers shirt on their turf), and listening to the riots (celebration?) in the streets after the game from my hotel room, I returned to New York with a sense of dread for Game Seven. Could the curse be lifted?

> "When the final seconds ticked off and the players started jumping up and down in celebration, a roar of ecstasy rose up from the fans."

The energy in the Garden that night was raucous, intense. It felt like every single person in there was on the edge of their seats from the start of the national anthem. It was as if 18,200 people had a collective knot in their stomachs for three hours, back and forth we went from joy to dread as goals were scored for and against the Rangers. My good friend, Frank, who had flown in with me from Vancouver, left at one point and came back with a mini Stanley Cup souvenir. I viewed this as an unlucky talisman and made him renounce it and throw it away. We were dealing with a fifty-four-year-old curse and only the collective focus and energy of everyone in that arena could lift it. The score was too close to get cocky. No premature cups!

In the end there are some that say that it was the spirit of Ceil Saidel, a longtime season ticket holder, who had recently died that made the difference that night. The Garden had kept her seat empty that night out of respect and tribute to her. I would like to think that they also kept it empty to let her spirit know that we wouldn't want her to miss the game. I believe she was there that night and may well have been the deciding factor. It takes a lot to lift a curse.

When the final seconds ticked off and the players started jumping up and down in celebration, a roar of ecstasy rose up from the fans. The collective joy in the Garden that night was unlike anything I had ever experienced or will likely experience again. So many years of broken hearts were mended in that moment. One fan held up a sign that said "Now I can die in peace." The captain held the grail above his head. The cup was ours.

OPPOSITE
June 14, 1994 – The captain carries The Cup.

"You can feel the energy the minute you step inside the building. It is, without a doubt, The World's Most Famous Arena."

– MARK MESSIER

LEFT
Brian Leetch's legacy includes two Norris Trophies, the 1994 Conn Smythe Trophy, and ten All-Star Game appearances.

RIGHT
July 13, 2000 – Three years after departing for Vancouver, Mark Messier returned to the Blueshirts.

February 4, 2004 – Mike Richter's #35 heads for the rafters.

Christopher Reeve

Gretzky's Last Stand

April 18, 1999. A date scarcely noticed or long forgotten by many. For others, including me, not only was it a date to remember but a moment in time that endures because we remember exactly where we were. It didn't matter that the Rangers had just lost to Pittsburgh. A sold-out crowd of more than 18,000 people were on their feet in the semi-darkness of the arena, cheering at the top of their lungs as one man took another easy lap around the rink in the glare of a dozen spotlights. It was the day that Number 99, Wayne Gretzky, retired.

I was lucky enough to be there. With my wife Dana, my seven-year-old son Will and his friend Penn on either side of me, I sat parked in my wheelchair next to the ice where the Zamboni and the visiting teams enter. Scores of guests, friends, and Garden staff pressed in behind us. Now the Great One was smiling shyly and waving to the crowd on his third encore, and still they didn't want to let him go.

"The Great One was named first, second, and third star of the game. With an assist to Brian Leetch he racked up the final point of his career."

Memories of brief connections with Gretzky came to mind as we watched. When Will was a Mite in a junior hockey league, he played in a brief exhibition game at the Garden. Wayne came over, stood beside me for a while, and then said, "Your son looks good. Nice shot." In January 1999 Wayne not only participated with the Rangers in a fundraiser for the Christopher Reeve Paralysis Foundation, but he joined me in a TV spot to promote it. Every time I went into the locker room after a game Wayne would come over to greet me and shake hands with all the awestruck friends and kids who tagged along.

The day of April 18, 1999 Gretzky signed sticks with #99 for all his teammates. Before the puck dropped, singer John Amirante changed the words in the national anthem from "land of the free" to "land of Wayne Gretzky." The Great One was named first, second, and third star of the game. With an assist to Brian Leetch he racked up the final point of his career.

Now the last lap was nearly over. Hundreds of hats still littered the ice after Gretzky had graciously put some on his head. He had passed by both benches and shaken hands or spoken to the players, coaches, and officials. Still waving to the crowd, he glided behind the net to round the corner.

And then came the moment frozen in time. He stopped by the Zamboni entrance and thanked us for being there. He patted Will on the shoulder, kissed Dana on the cheek, and then leaned over to give me a quick embrace. The next instant he had moved on and we haven't seen him since.

No matter. We were there for one of the great moments in the fabled history of Madison Square Garden.

OPPOSITE
April 18, 1999 – The Great One says goodbye.

POLITICAL CONVENTIONS

Governor Mario Cuomo

An Honor and a Privilege

Madison Square Garden is one of the great symbols of New York, like the Statue of Liberty and the Empire State Building. As soon as you see any of these structures the words that come to mind are "New York." That made the 1992 Democratic National Convention held at the Garden really special.

Two weeks before the Convention the late Ron Brown, a former law school student of mine who was the Chairman of the Democratic National Committee, asked me to make the nominating speech for Bill Clinton. I thought they needed someone who had more heft and a bigger footprint in the party, so I said no. Both Ron and Governor Clinton pressed the point and so I agreed to give the speech, but with reluctance.

"Moments like that you don't deserve. Moments like that are given to you as gifts for reasons you'll never fully understand. And they stay with you forever."

In preparing speeches, I don't worry much about words; I worry a lot about ideas and whether they will make sense to the audience. They have to be ideas that are clear, cogent and appeal immediately. I worked hard trying to find them, analyzing what President Bush had done and failed to do that left the economy in such bad condition, and what Bill Clinton could do better. Before I ever started writing any words and full sentences, I wrote outline after outline, trying to get the logic right. Then, three days before the event I wrote the words into a speech. Up to the very day of the speech I continued to make changes because every time I read it I had another thought, another nuance. On the very last day at the hotel, just hours before the speech, I changed half a page.

The idea of being at Madison Square Garden, surrounded with so many people in this great arc in front of you, all trying to deal with one of the most important decisions a democracy must make, was awesome. When I thought that millions of people, far beyond the Garden, would also be listening and their decisions as to who should be President of the United States might be influenced by my words, if only a little bit, I was troubled that I might not be able to do the occasion justice. I knew that what I was doing was only a very small part of our campaign, but nonetheless it mattered and that, to me, created a very heavy responsibility, and a high degree of anxiety. I uttered a silent prayer "Please, Oh Lord, please, just one time, give me twenty-five minutes without blowing it, don't let me lose my train of thought, let me get this thing done, reasonably well, because we need Bill Clinton as President."

In preparing myself, I had remembered some early experiences at Madison Square Garden. During one, I was participating in a high school basketball game for St. John's Prep. I was playing what you would call today the shooting guard position. Our point guard came down with four or five seconds left on the clock before halftime — I'll never forget this. He paused at what would today be beyond the college three-point line and

PREVIOUS SPREAD
July 1992 – The Democrats hold court at
the Garden for the first time since 1980.

ABOVE
July 16, 1992 – Bill Clinton and Al Gore
accept the 1992 Democratic nomination.

ABOVE
June 1924 – The Democratic Convention at Garden II
turned into a two-week marathon that ultimately
produced the nomination of John W. Davis.

"The main thing is, 'Never quit,
never quit, never quit.'"

— BILL CLINTON, 1992 DEMOCRATIC CONVENTION

looked up at the basket. I yelled "Don't shoot!" — I thought it was too early to shoot. As I shouted "Don't shoot!" — loud enough so the few hundred people in the Garden could all hear me — he let the ball go and the darn thing went in!

I didn't want to make another mistake like that one! Especially not at a major convention in a presidential year as the nominating speaker.

In 1992 we knew the United States could do better than it had been doing. New York was vital to the effort to make the changes we needed. As Governor of New York, I was given a chance to urge America to vote for the one person I knew could help us make those changes. The decision as to President was a lot more important than shouting at a point guard not to shoot in a high school game; now I could shout at a whole Garden full of people — and millions watching and listening — saying — "Look, we have a champion here who can bring us a lot closer to our goals as a people than we're going to get if we don't make a change."

There was something thrilling about that. It was a great honor to be chosen by the Democratic Party and the man who was going to be President to make the case for him. I'll never forget it.

My feeling about the few moments like that in my life was always the same. Secretly I said to myself, "What am I doing here? How did I get here?" I never for a moment fooled myself into thinking "This is something I really deserve." It never was: moments like that you don't deserve. Moments like that are given to you as gifts for reasons you'll never fully understand. And they stay with you forever.

The night in the Garden in 1992...how sweet it was!

LEFT
August 1980 – Un-conventional behavior?

RIGHT
July 15, 1976 – En route to the White House,
Jimmy Carter got the nod from the Democrats.

ABOVE
August 1980 – An off-camera moment for
CBS's Walter Cronkite.

SPORTING EVENTS

John McEnroe

From the Rafters to Center Stage (and Back Again)

When I first started attending Rangers and Knicks games at age eight, I sat with my father in the blue seats. For people who don't know the Garden, the seats were color-coded, and at the time, the blue seats formed the upper level. They were the seats furthest from the action, and were often referred to as the "cheap" seats. Yes, my connection to the Garden started upstairs.

Growing up in New York, the Garden always symbolized "making it" to me. If you could compete there, you had become one of the best at your sport.

After watching games from afar as a child, I was fortunate to have the opportunity to compete at the Garden in a major tennis tournament at a very young age. In 1977, when I was just eighteen years old, I reached the semi-finals of Wimbledon. About a year later, I turned professional and by the end of 1978 I had become one of the top eight players in the world, and earned the right to participate in the Masters, which was held at the Garden.

"Growing up in New York, the Garden always symbolized 'making it' to me. If you could compete there, you had become one of the best at your sport."

I was still living at home on Long Island with my parents, but during the event I stayed at The Plaza, the tournament hotel. "This is going to be incredible," I said to myself. Of course, when I saw my room, I exclaimed, "It's as big as our kitchen table."

For me, it was an unforgettable tournament. In the round-robin portion of the event, I played my nemesis, Jimmy Connors, to whom I had lost the first four times we played. I was determined to beat him. I won the first set and was winning 3-0 in the second when Connors defaulted! He said he had blisters. This guy wasn't going to give me the satisfaction of winning. But I put up my hands in victory anyway. The hell with the blisters, a win's a win, I thought to myself.

In the finals, I played Arthur Ashe. Having beaten Arthur 6-2, 6-3 in the round-robin, I was expecting that the match would be a breeze. But Arthur changed his strategy. He started slicing and dicing, mixing things up, and I had a hard time combating his off-speed tactics. Before I knew it, he was up 5-3, 40-15 in the third set, and at double match-point. I was ready to pull my hair out, and at that point I had lots of hair! Somehow I pulled myself together and won the match. I had started to learn to dig deep inside myself, something that would become a signature of my career.

PREVIOUS SPREAD
March 23, 1973 – After captivating the world
at the Munich Olympics, Russian gymnast
Olga Korbut played the Garden.

LEFT
John McEnroe exulted as he won the 1979 Masters.

RIGHT
From wonder in the blue seats to anguish
at center court, John McEnroe ran the gamut
of Garden emotion.

"This is, I believe to be, the
greatest arena in the world."

— STEFFI GRAF

A couple of years later, in the second set tie-break of a sold-out round-robin match at the Garden against Bjorn Borg, I'll never forget seeing Borg do something that at the time was unheard of: he questioned a call. Up until then, Borg had said about two words in his entire career. When he disagreed with the umpire during our match, I didn't know whether to feel embarrassed or proud. I guess I could bring out the best and worst in opponents, and at least I'd like to think that I provided good entertainment and gave the fans their money's worth.

At Madison Square Garden, the unexpected becomes the norm. During one of my matches against Guillermo Vilas, a man came up behind me during a change-over and tapped me on the shoulder. I was surprised, because nobody ever comes up to a player during a change-over. I tried to ignore him, and was about to explode, when I looked up and saw it was Ronnie Wood of the Rolling Stones! "Hey, John, I just wanted to say hello," he said. Seeing him provided me with such a jolt of adrenaline that I didn't miss a ball for an hour.

I'll never forget my last victory at the Garden. It was January 1985, and I beat Ivan Lendl in the Masters Final, in one of the best matches of my career. Everything was clicking at that point, but sadly, for me, I never won there again, and even worse, the tournament was moved to Germany in 1990.

I've actually done more than play tennis at the Garden; I've also played guitar, my favorite pastime, there. Chrissy Hynde, lead singer of the Pretenders, asked me to sit in on a song when the Pretenders opened for the Stones in 2002. I feared the crowd would boo me because of my mediocre guitar skills, but instead they cheered like mad. And I never had to hit an ace during the entire performance!

After September 11th, it was apparent to many of us that the real heroes aren't the athletes and rock stars who compete and perform at the Garden, but the police, firefighters, and emergency service workers who put their lives on the line every day. I had befriended a group of firefighters and wanted to go to a Rangers game with them. The Garden gave us a bunch of tickets, and in December 2001 we went, sitting in the upper deck, in a section called Hometown Heroes. It had been ages since I'd sat up there, and in returning to those seats, I came to a realization.

These are the true fans that give the Garden its character. These fans pay their hard-earned money, and they've got the worst seats in the house, yet they seem to love it more than anyone. They are the most devoted, the most vocal, and the most faithful fans. I really appreciated the fact that the Garden, a place where so many athletic and cultural legends had played, was now host to these real heroes, giving them their own well-deserved section.

The Garden has always been a special place for me. The Garden crowd lifts you up—win, lose, or draw. Remember, I'm from New York. That's my home-court advantage.

ABOVE
The determined face of a champion:
Venus Williams.

TOP
Steffi Graf captured five singles titles in her Garden career.

BOTTOM
Jimmy Connors, always a crowd favorite, at the Volvo Masters.

Peggy Fleming

Connecting with the Audience

Skating at Madison Square Garden was always special for me. After I won the Olympics in 1968, I started performing in the Ice Follies across the nation. When the Ice Follies reached New York, the Garden offered glamour as well as media exposure. But I realized early on that what makes performing at the Garden special was actually the audience.

The reaction of the crowd at the Garden was different than at any other venue. They really appreciated our more thoughtful performances, and the classical musical went over better there. Garden audiences always knew when to applaud and when to hold back. The audience in New York was always attentive, educated, and appreciative. At the same time, performing at the Garden was more stressful than appearing anywhere else. Since so much of the media is concentrated in New York, the reviews of the Ice Follies could go a long way to establishing your reputation and determining whether or not the show was a success. That made everyone nervous; we had to perform our absolute best, at the highest quality, to generate good reviews. But we knew if we could win over the New York critics, we'd be a success.

Skating at the Garden, I felt alone on the ice but also attuned to the crowd. Because of the way the stands extend out from the main floor, I was aware that people were watching, but felt the crowd was at a distance at the same time. I was focused on my movement, but aware of the audience, whether they were applauding wildly or holding their breath. Though I was performing in an arena that holds more than 18,000 people, I felt the intimacy of the Garden and could sense the crowd's reaction to every twist and turn.

Garden audiences could be boisterous and expressive, or quiet and totally attentive. Even when the audience was quiet it meant they were totally immersed in what I was doing. I could always sense whether the crowd was with me or not.

Performing at the Garden had another unique aspect. The ceiling lights at the Garden are arranged in a circle, following the form of the building, rather than running straight across the ceiling, as at other arenas. When I was executing a lay-back spin or other moves, I found myself beginning to get dizzy. After spinning around, I'd have to remind myself where the arena's front or back was located. But after performing at many ice shows at the Garden, I gradually adjusted to the lights.

Skating at the Garden could be magical. For "Some Enchanted Evening," I wore a long white gown that almost touched the ice. We choreographed the number around the dress, which billowed out more beautifully when I was skating forward than backward. Skating moves are quick, but the chiffon filled the spotlight and made the movements linger. The crowd was enrapt at every move.

Winning the Olympics in 1968 was the crowning achievement of my career. At the closing ceremony, I had skated to "Ave Maria" in honor of my father, who had died two years earlier. He loved that particular piece of music and I've had the opportunity to perform it numerous times over the years at the Garden, to thunderous applause.

OPPOSITE
At the 1968 Olympics and beyond, Peggy Fleming personified beauty and grace.

TOP
Dorothy Hamill enchanted the world as both Olympic gold medallist and show-stopping professional.

BELOW LEFT
Charles T. Church presents Sonja Henie with her trophy after she won the 1930 World Figure Skating Championship at the Garden.

BELOW RIGHT
Scott Hamilton, ever the showman.

Bart Conner **Gymnastics Comes of Age**

GYMNASTICS

When Madison Square Garden hosted its first major gymnastics event in 1976 — the American Cup — the sport gained instant credibility.

The Garden also symbolized my coming of age. This was the arena where I made a name for myself, celebrated my eighteenth birthday, and met my future wife, Nadia Comaneci, whom I married twenty years later. For me, the Garden offered more than a scrapbook of memories; it's where I experienced my life's most defining moments.

I was a kid from the suburbs of Chicago when I entered the Garden for the first time, at seventeen, to compete in the American Cup. I vividly recall the sights and sounds of that day. I remember the smell of beer permeating the arena, and all the gymnasts being herded together into a freight elevator, known for transporting the elephants in the circus. Perhaps we gymnasts had not "arrived" as much as we thought!

"For me, the Garden offered more than a scrapbook of memories; it's where I experienced my life's most defining moments."

The Garden was a beehive of activity during the day, since it was used for multiple events within a matter of hours. Indeed, that day we practiced on parallel bars and springboards at the Felt Forum, because the main arena was presenting basketball in the afternoon and hockey at night. When we finally made it to the main arena to practice, we almost froze: the gym floor was placed atop the ice, and since gymnasts run around in socks, our feet were turning into icicles.

I was competing against my boyhood idol, Mitsuo Tsukahara, the Japanese Olympic Gold medallist from 1972. I couldn't sleep the night before because I was so excited about competing. In addition, the noise outside my Statler Hilton hotel room, across the street from the Garden, was keeping me awake.

Bubbling over with energy, I went to warm up for two hours before the event, practicing and refining all of my routines. When I sauntered into the locker room, I spotted Tsukahara, who by then was in his thirties. He was sitting on a bench, dressed in his warm-up suit, smoking a cigarette and sipping coffee. When I asked him if he was going to practice, he replied, "At my age, I can either warm up or compete." On the last day of competition, I beat my idol.

Not only did I win, but I also celebrated my eighteenth birthday on March 28. The entire crowd serenaded me with "Happy Birthday." I was holding the Silver Cup trophy, standing next to the fourteen-year-old phenom, Nadia Comaneci, the Romanian gymnast who would, within months, go on to win three gold medals at the Montreal Olympics. Nadia had launched her mission toward an Olympic gold medal at that

OPPOSITE
March 28, 1976 – Prior to scoring seven perfect 10s at the 1976 Olympics, Nadia Comaneci competed at the American Cup at the Garden, and met a destiny of another kind.

TOP
Bart Conner on the high bar.

BOTTOM
Mary Lou Retton, America's star-spangled medallist.

Garden meet. She scored a perfect 10 on one of her vaults — the first gymnast ever to achieve that — setting the stage for what she would accomplish later that summer at the Olympics. As we stood there together, one of the photographers suggested that I kiss her, and that picture of us circulated the globe. Little did I know then that twenty years later, in a special ceremony in Bucharest, Romania, Nadia and I would be married.

Years later, when Nadia and I were on a talk show together, the host asked when we had met. Nadia said it was in 1981, but I reminded her it was actually five years earlier. "Nadia, don't you remember in the Garden, when I kissed you on the cheek?" I asked. "That was a little blonde guy," she retorted. "That was me," I told her. Of course, she was fourteen, and she was so committed to her gymnastics that she was focused on the vaults, not on her fellow gymnasts.

Olga Korbut, the gold medal winner for gymnastics in the 1972 Munich Games, had ignited interest in gymnastics. But it was Nadia who really put the sport on the map. When she burst onto the scene four years later, no one had ever seen a gymnast who was so single-minded in her focus. She was fearless, and all business.

In 1976, I won the meet, celebrated my eighteenth birthday, and met my future bride. People talk about the wonder of performing at the Garden. But for me, competing at the Garden turned out to be a life-defining experience.

ABOVE
March 23, 1973 – Olga Korbut on the balance beam.

Bill Cosby

How Did He Do That?

When I first started going to Madison Square Garden, they allowed smoking, so your eyes had to cut through thick cigar, pipe, and cigarette smoke to see anything. But I still managed to witness some wonderful sports moments over the years. Here, in no particular chronological order, are a few of them.

I saw great fighters like Roberto Duran. And I was at the first Ali-Frazier fight. Ringside seats. I was there with my wife Camille and with Clarence Williams III of *Mod Squad* before *Mod Squad* became a huge hit. At some point during this fantastic boxing match, a fistfight broke out in the audience and I found it very interesting that people turned to watch two lousy fighters in street clothes who kept missing each other but somehow started bleeding from places they weren't hit.

"What Barksdale did — which became known as an 'unorthodox scissors kick' — was incredible to watch."

There was college basketball in the fifties. The New York area colleges were extremely competitive in those days. Long Island University. New York University. St. John's. Manhattan College. CCNY. And two hands were very important at that time, two-handed chest pass, two-handed set shot. (Which today would probably cause a lot of headaches for the shooter, from having the shot blocked and the ball bouncing off the forehead, rendering the shooter cockeyed.)

I once played basketball in the Garden with the Harlem Globetrotters, wearing a Harlem Globetrotters uniform. I think I set a record of sorts, being the only Globetrotter to ever go oh-for-six and get booed by little children.

Track and field has always been big at the Garden. Two events I love so much that I never leave early are the Millrose Games and the Colgate Games. I'll never forget the Colgate Games, with all those youngsters pumping elbows around the track. And the Millrose Games are sort of like a three-ring circus, with so much going on in the infield: male judges in tuxedos, women judges in business attire, sprinters exploding for sixty meters, then splatting into a protective mat hanging over an exit.

One of my heroes, and I don't recall why, because this race was not a race I ever wanted to train for or run, was Reginald (Reggie) Pearlman, who ran the 880 for NYU and later the New York Athletic Club. I think I liked him because of those dark-rimmed glasses that were taped to his face while he was running. Reggie always woke up the New York fans when he entered the track. Also, there was Roscoe Lee Brown, who ran as Roscoe Brown. Running for the New York Pioneer Club in 1952, Roscoe won the 880 at the Millrose Games in a time of 1:56.7.

But the most unusual sight I have ever seen was Bob Barksdale of Morgan State competing in the high jump. At that time high jumpers would run to the bar, kick one leg into the air, roll over the bar facing down, then

OPPOSITE
February 12, 1956 – Bob Barksdale's unique
high-jump style made a lasting impression.

148

ABOVE
February 9, 1968 – In the last track meet
at Garden III, Jim Ryun ran the mile in a
sterling 3:57.5.

land in the pit on their backs. Not Barksdale. I have never seen a style like his in my life. There were some Japanese jumpers, who were usually gymnasts, and they would do a couple back flips over the bar, but then the third jump would be disqualified because, in those days, you couldn't go over the bar head first. But even these inventive Japanese jumpers never dared to try what Barksdale did. Nor have I ever heard of any coach stepping forward and saying: I am the inventor of Barksdale's high jump style.

What Barksdale did — which became known as an "unorthodox scissors kick" — was incredible to watch. He would run to the bar, swing his leg up, and then somehow position himself with his back facing the bar, like a drunk lying on a flophouse mattress.

After watching Barksdale, I traveled back to Philadelphia and, being a high jumper, decided to try this style of jumping. I set the height at four feet eleven inches. Then I ran toward the bar, approaching from the right side; planted my left foot, kicking upward with my right leg so my body rose in a sitting position; rotated my right leg over the bar, raised my arm so that it cleared the bar at the same time as my right leg, kept

my back straight, and brought my left leg up. The speed carried me over the bar and into the pit face first. Splat! I tried this method three of four times and always hurt myself. Obviously, I abandoned this style, but today, at age sixty-six, there is a small muscle in the area of the coccyx and lumbar region, which still hurts me whenever I see Bob Barksdale walking around Madison Square Garden in a tuxedo. I recently talked to a lawyer about suing him, but he told me the statute of limitations had expired. Meanwhile, Bob Barksdale seems to walk just fine.

BOTTOM
For a decade, the Wanamaker Mile at the Millrose Games was the private province of the great Eamonn Coghlan.

TOP
January 31, 1959 – John Thomas, a seventeen-year-old Boston University student, cleared seven feet in the high jump, the first time this feat was accomplished at an indoor meet.

"For me, it all started at Madison Square Garden."

– JACKIE JOYNER-KERSEE

TOP
February, 1980 – Earl Bell won the pole vault
at the Millrose Games with a vault of 18'-0".

BOTTOM
February 6, 2004 – Marion Jones (second
from left) won the 60-meter dash at the
2004 Millrose Games.

OPPOSITE
February, 1988 – Jackie Joyner-Kersee
in the long jump at the Millrose Games.

Mary Tyler Moore

Of Dogs and Dreams

Imagine ladies and gentlemen in their gowns and tuxedos, dogs resplendent and groomed, and finally the proud handlers parading their dogs, as the green carpet has been rolled out, all hoping to receive the colored ribbons awarded for "Best in Show." This is the Westminster Kennel Club Dog Show, under the magnificent ceiling of Madison Square Garden — indisputably "America's Dog Show" — and the biggest in the world.

The Westminster Kennel Club Dog Show derived its name from the sporting gentlemen who frequented the Westminster Hotel in New York, and started the dog show in 1877. It has become America's second-longest continuous sporting event, second by only one year to the Kentucky Derby. This truly unique affair has glamour, elegance, and poise, ever-present in both the contestants and their owners—but it really *is* the dogs' night. All of the dogs are class acts as they strut their stuff with the carriage and demeanor of champions. Just to be in this show makes you a winner: each dog is a star. And this prestigious event is a celebration of the wonderful canine spirit, reflecting our emotional and spiritual attachments to our dogs.

For my husband and me, this show has had a wonderful impact on our lives, and actually contributed to our obtaining two dogs of our own. We discovered a way to acquire dogs while not contributing to the problem of overpopulation: at the show we learned that some breeders take in dogs that need a home and advertise on the Internet. After conducting an Internet search, we acquired Shadow, a Golden Retriever, through Yankee Golden Retriever Rescue and Shana, our Miniature Schnauzer, via New Jersey Schnauzer.

Golden Retrievers are my favorite breed. Unlike any other breed, they possess a special intelligence. Increasingly, Golden Retrievers (as well as Labradors) are being used as guide dogs for the blind. They're so intelligent that blind people can always depend on them for assistance. I also like schnauzers, but they can be arrogant. Shana acts like a princess: she rules the roost at home, and often wants revenge when Shadow gets his way.

While I love attending the Westminster show, I cringed when I learned there that New York City destroys more than 35,000 dogs a year. That's criminal, and something should be done to change it! In fact, the Westminster Dog Show encourages people to take better care of their canines and not abandon them. And at the dog show, you see how valuable, gracious, and beautiful these animals are.

Unfortunately, I never got to attend any events at the Garden when I was a child. While I was born in Brooklyn and raised in Flushing, Queens until I was nine, my entire family moved to Los Angeles when my uncle, a successful theatrical agent, convinced us to move to California. My relationship with the Garden began when I returned to New York in the early 1980s and got to know the acclaimed choreographer Jacques d'Amboise.

OPPOSITE
Best in Show was won by Chinoe's Adamant James, an English Springer Spaniel, two years in a row — 1971 and 1972.

D'Amboise, a great dancer with the New York City Ballet, started the nonprofit National Dance Institute in 1976 to train urban youth in the fourth through the sixth grades in dance and the arts. Each year, he choreographs a year-end event for the National Dance Institute, with 1,200 New York City students. Several times this event has taken place at the Garden.

Jacques asked me to participate in his dances at the Garden, and of course, since I love dance, I couldn't resist. Nor will I ever forget the roles he assigned me. In the first ballet, I was a tap-dancing duck in a ballet about China (you won't find this role on my résumé, I'll admit!), and in the second, I danced as a New York City cop, performing with real policemen and policewomen.

Dancing has always played a special role in my life. I took dancing lessons as a child and always dreamed about becoming a ballerina. More than anything else in the world, I wanted to be a dancer. Despite my success as an actress in the *Mary Tyler Moore Show* and in films such as *Ordinary People*, sometimes it occurs to me that, when I go to my grave, I will think of myself not as a successful actress, but as a failed dancer.

ABOVE
Bob Wolff, whose broadcasting career has spanned six decades, included thirty-two years with the Westminster Kennel Club Dog Show. Wolff helped popularize the show with his off-beat sense of humor.

TOP
February 10, 2004 – Best in Show 2004 was won by
Darbydale's All Rise Pouchcove, a Newfoundland owned
by Peggy Helming and Carol A. Bernard Bergmann.

BOTTOM
Lots of preparation precedes every competition.

Lorraine Bracco

A Place Where Dreams Come True

When my daughter Stella was eleven, she begged me to take her to the National Horse Show at Madison Square Garden. "Mommy," she said, squeezing my hand, "this is a dream for me. I'd like to learn to ride horses." Seeing your child inspired with such a dream is a wonderful thing to behold.

We didn't know at the outset where riding would take Stella, but it's been a journey well worth the effort. Watching her work hard and focus on a goal has been inspiring. Having improved her riding skills through lessons and practice, Stella now competes in jumpers, equitation, and hunter. She's had her share of role models along the way, including Margie Engel, the Olympic rider, and her friends Georgina Bloomberg (Mayor Bloomberg's daughter), and Daisy Johnson, who have competed at the National Horse Show.

My own connection to the Garden began when I was a fifteen-year-old high school student on Long Island. When a friend offered me a ticket for the Concert for Bangladesh, I had to ask my parents' permission to go into the city at by train at night. As many of us know, taking the Long Island Railroad into the Garden by yourself is a rite of passage.

> "When my daughter Stella was eleven, she begged me to take her to the National Horse Show at Madison Square Garden."

Imagine what it was like for a high-school student to have her first Garden experience attending the ground-breaking Concert for Bangladesh. This concert wasn't only about music: it raised awareness about giving to people who were needy and less fortunate, and paved the way for many other musical benefits. Listening to great musicians such as George Harrison and Ravi Shankar, surrounded by 18,500 fans that wanted to change the world through their own generosity was an experience I'll never forget. I still remember Harrison coming out in a white suit and orange shirt. To this Long Island teenager, he looked great. I remember the announcer saying, "And we have another friend who is here to perform," and Bob Dylan ambled onto the stage.

Since I was fifteen, Madison Square Garden and I have been constant companions. At a Rolling Stones concert, I was lucky enough to sit behind the stage and see Mick Jagger and the band at work. As a boxing fan, I've been to several of Lennox Lewis's fights at the Garden. And on October 20, 2001, I attended the Concert for New York City to honor our true "heroes" of the city.

Ever since I've been playing psychiatrist Dr. Jennifer Melfi on HBO's hit series *The Sopranos*, Knicks fans stop me when I'm attending games. Many people tell me that Dr. Melfi has played a role in helping make psychiatry more acceptable and removing the stigma from it. That makes me feel good.

Having attained a modicum of celebrity, I also have gotten to sit at courtside seats during Knicks games, which I love. You feel as if you're totally in the game! The first time I sat at courtside, I sat next to Billy Crystal, and asked him what the proper etiquette was for sitting in these seats. "Lean back," he replied, cracking me up.

Boxing did get me into trouble with my mom one time, though. My father accompanied me to the Evander Holyfield–Lennox Lewis match in 1999. Fights, of course, start late and end late. When my dad arrived home at four in the morning, my mother wanted to know why he had come home right before breakfast. We told her that the energy at the fight was electric, and we just had to attend the after-fight parties.

Athletes aspire to compete at Madison Square Garden just as performers dream about playing there. And just like my daughter dreams about riding at the National Horse Show.

ABOVE
The National Horse Show had a long history at the Garden, starting in 1883.

GLOBETROTTERS

TOP
The Harlem Globetrotters have entertained millions of fans for more than three-quarters of a century, with the antics of Bill Cosby (L) and Meadowlark Lemon (R) making the Garden crowd roar with laughter.

BOTTOM
1981 – Curly Neal (L) and Geese Ausbie (R) gave a young fan a memory that will last a lifetime.

Globetrotter Curly Neal showed the referee how
it's done.

Chris Jericho

WRESTLING

Raised at the Garden

My first memory of the Garden was that the fans were too loud. I was only three years old, and I was there with my mom, watching my dad play hockey. My father, Ted Irvine, played for the Rangers from 1970-1975 and I watched him play many times, but that doesn't mean I liked it. I was always angry with him, because while he was in the heat of battle, he never had the courtesy to take his eyes off the puck, look up in the stands, and wave hello to me. My mother explained that he was busy trying to win the game, but that never made much sense to my young mind. If *I* were playing, I would certainly have waved hello and smiled, I thought. After all, he was my daddy.

As if being snubbed by my father wasn't bad enough, I was also forced to put up with the constant barrage of sound assaulting my ears. The fans at the Garden were rabid, merciless, passionate — and very vocal. (They still are.) I remember pulling the sweater that my grandma had knitted for me, emblazoned with the face of a New York Ranger, over my head in an attempt to drown out the sound. Of course, it never worked.

But it was those memories that instilled the desire to someday perform at the Garden myself. I'd been wrestling for nine years before I made my Garden debut, shortly after I made my World Wrestling Entertainment (WWE) entrance. It was one of the most exciting moments of my career, and a true milestone for me. I wanted to make an impact, to set the tone for my WWE career, and make sure the New York wrestling fans would never forget me. I was scheduled to do an interview that night, and I was nervous and excited as I walked into the ring. I made my way through the ropes, grabbed the microphone, looked at the assembled Jericho-holics in attendance and started to utter my opening words. Much to my dismay, the microphone cut out and died. I almost did, too.

Thankfully, my Garden experiences have gone steadily uphill since then, and I've had some great moments and great matches. I've headlined Pay-Per-Views, starred in *Monday Night Raw*, participated in SuperSkate — the Rangers' annual celebrity charity hockey game that benefits the team's Cheering for Children Foundation and the Christopher Reeve Paralysis Foundation — and entertained tens of thousands of the best wrestling fans in the world.

But my favorite Garden memory occurred when I played in my third SuperSkate event, against one Ted Irvine. I flew my dad in to play the game, on the condition that he would be on the opposing team. Standing across the blue line from him during the national anthem was one of the greatest moments of my life. Getting beaten up by him (I let him win, naturally), during a fight later in the game was a different story.

As a matter of fact, I've been beaten up by a veritable smorgasbord of opponents at the Garden — from The Rock, RVD, and Stone Cold Steve Austin in the WWE, to Dennis Leary, Boomer Esiason, and David Boreanaz at the charity games. But I did it to entertain the Garden brethren, and I will continue to do so because they are the loudest and best fans in the world.

And I'd like to think that at some point during one of my performances in New York City, a three-year-old kid had to pull his sweater over his head because the crowd was too loud.

OPPOSITE
March 31, 1985 – The Garden hosted the first
WrestleMania® with Champion Hulk Hogan. Hogan
and Mr. T took on Rowdy Roddy Piper and Paul
"Mr. Wonderful" Orndorff.

BOTTOM
March 31, 1985 – Cyndi Lauper in the ring at
WrestleMania® I. Lauper served as Wendi Richter's
manager, and under Lauper's guidance, Richter
defeated Lelani Kai for the Women's Championship.

TOP
March 14, 2004 – Leap of Faith
Shawn Michaels threw caution to the wind as he
executed a moonsault onto Triple H and Chris Benoit
at WrestleMania® XX.

SPORTING EVENTS

TOP
1939 – Six-day bike races were held at Gardens I, II, and III beginning in 1898. Teams cycled around the track non-stop, and one team member always had to be on the track. Here, Yankee star Joe DiMaggio started the race.

BOTTOM
October 6, 1942 – The Rodeo — starring Roy Rogers, "King of the Cowboys," and his famous horse Trigger — visited the Garden.

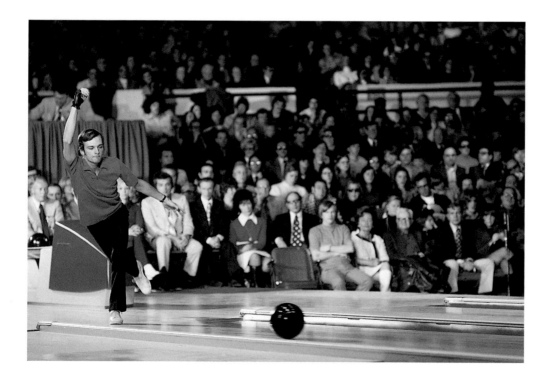

BOTTOM
January 8, 1972 – From the late 1960s through the late 1980s, the Madison Square Garden Bowling Center included a 48-lane bowling alley. Don Johnson, nicknamed the "Kokomo Kid," bowled his way to victory in the 1972 BPAA US Open.

TOP
Roller Derby returned to the Garden in the 1970s, with the New York Chiefs renewing their seemingly endless rivalry with the T-Birds and the Bay Area Bombers.

TOP
The Garden was home field for the
CityHawks, an arena football team, during
the summers of 1997 and 1998. Mike Perez
was the quarterback.

BOTTOM
February 1973 – The Yamaha Silver Cup
was held at the Garden.

RIGHT
The Felt Forum hosted the Ms. Olympia
body-building championships for several
years in the 1980s.

BOTTOM
From Buffalo Bill Cody's Wild West Show to Roy Rogers
to contemporary professional events, rodeo has a long
history at the Garden.

TOP
February 1984 – Monster trucks took over the arena.

Al Trautwig ## Made for TV

As legend has it, sometime in 1980, Sonny Werblin, the flamboyant chief of Madison Square Garden at the time, summoned his executives to discuss marketing at the Garden. He decided they would call it "The World's Most Famous Arena." To this day, the Garden is still called "The World's Most Famous Arena" by fans, the media, and players, because the nickname still applies; it has withstood the test of time. And one of the primary reasons it applies is television. Think about it; for Madison Square Garden to really be known around the world, something had to take the aura of the building beyond its walls to a worldwide audience craving entertainment.

From the first Garden building through the fourth, the mantra has remained the same: give people a reason to come. Initially it was the circus, later it was bicycle races, but the major developments were the formation of the NHL in 1926 and the NBA twenty years later. That gave the Garden inventory. All that had to be done then was to wait for technology to catch up with what the Garden had to offer. That started in 1939: newly-created television stations needed content to fill the time, attract viewers, and give people a reason to buy TV sets.

"From the first Garden building through the fourth, the mantra has remained the same: give people a reason to come."

Three days after the first sporting event was televised — a 1939 Columbia-Princeton baseball game — a cycling event was broadcast from the Garden. The next year the first-ever hockey game aired on Channel W2XBS (now WCBS), and the list of firsts after that was long and memorable. Madison Square Garden had been an important gathering place in America's largest city, but it reached new levels of fame when the current Garden was built in 1968.

The ceiling was a big part of the new Garden's identity. It distinguished the Garden from any other arena. Every other venue had a standard mix of girders and lights that made them all look the same. But the moment you turned on a televised event from the Garden you knew where it was being held. The lighting. The buzzer. The voice of the public address announcer, John Condon. The best athletes, and most talented performers, found their way to the Garden. Careers were being defined at the Garden.

Ali versus Frazier reached a worldwide audience. A Jethro Tull concert was beamed from there back to the United Kingdom. Political conventions and other significant cultural events were televised and, as a result, enhanced the stature of the Garden. In New York, cable television had grown enough by 1969 that the Garden could support an entire channel, MSG Network, which featured Knicks and Rangers home games. In 1971, Time/Life exposed those same games to a national audience on their new channel, HBO.

OPPOSITE
May 8, 1970 – Marv Albert interviewed Walt Frazier
after the Knicks won their first championship.

CONCERTS

November 27, 1969 – The Rolling Stones make
their first New York appearance, playing to
a sold-out Garden.

ABOVE
December 25, 1967 – Judy Garland performed
to adoring fans.

George Kalinsky

The End of the Rainbow

It seems fitting that the performer who opened the Felt Forum had one of the most booming voices and striking stage presences in all of entertainment history: Judy Garland. Before Bob Hope and Bing Crosby launched the new Madison Square Garden arena, Judy Garland had debuted at the Felt Forum (now called the Theater at Madison Square Garden), for a one-week engagement. Sadly, it was her penultimate American performance.

"She dazzled the audience with her performance, and they gave her a standing ovation after the finale, cheering 'Judy, Judy, Judy, we love you!'"

Days before her show opened, I saw Judy sitting forlornly in the front row of the empty theatre. As the production staff milled around, preparing the stage, I heard Sid Luft, Judy's manager and ex-husband, using harsh words with her. I felt sympathy toward her and decided to sit close to her to offer some support. "Darling," she said to me, her eyes glazed over and watery, "could you come over here and help me up?" She had trouble walking on her own, and it seemed as if at this point in her life, the yellow brick road had led only to despair and sadness.

And yet, when Judy appeared on stage, many of her problems fell by the wayside. As she walked onstage to the tune of "Somewhere Over the Rainbow," she seemed composed. She dazzled the audience with her performance, and they gave her a standing ovation after the finale, cheering "Judy, Judy, Judy, we love you!" It was clear to me that Judy lived to be onstage and thrived on the love of the audience.

I spent a week taking photographs of her. Little did I know that I was documenting the final curtain on one of the twentieth century's greatest, and most troubled, artists.

BOTTOM
October 13, 1974 – Frank Sinatra's "The Main Event"
was broadcast live around the world.

TOP
1986 – Stevie Wonder played two nights
in the round.

ABOVE
June 9, 1972 – "The King" in the first of four sold-out shows. Elvis Presley's charisma and presence rocked the music world.

"It's great to be back here. This place is like a milepost on the road. There's a lot of history here and it's great that it hasn't changed."

– NEIL YOUNG

TOP
May 18, 1969 – Jimi Hendrix played the Garden.

BOTTOM
December 19, 1969 – Janis Joplin and the Kozmic Blues Band played the Garden; this would be the last time Joplin performed with Kozmic Blues, and the only time she performed here.

ABOVE
January 24, 1969 – Jim Morrison of the Doors in
the first of four sold-out concerts at the Felt Forum.

Billy Crystal **Two Unforgettable Nights**

The first time I walked into the new Madison Square Garden, I saw George Harrison from the twenty-sixth row, and the next time I walked into the building for a concert of that magnitude, I was onstage, singing "Let It Be" with Paul McCartney. What a difference thirty years can make, though both concerts had a tremendous impact on me and many others.

At the Concert for Bangladesh, in 1971, George Harrison brought musicians together to raise money and awareness for the starving refugees of that war-torn country. The Garden became a sanctuary for music and for this amazing cause. Everyone was equal; we felt as if we all possessed the same mind-set. A powerful feeling of helping people through music and loving, not hurting them with Agent Orange and B-52s, permeated the arena. Bob Dylan, Ringo Starr, and Ravi Shankar proved you could free people in humanitarian ways. It made perfect sense to my generation. Here was this one particular moment at a time in our country's history when we needed music, perhaps more than ever, to respond to the rage that was happening around us. It was magical; we were in the perfect setting for this outpouring of generosity, beauty, passion, and compassion.

When George Harrison came out, it was the first time most of us had seen a Beatle in person. It was mesmerizing! And the duet between Eric Clapton and George Harrison on "While My Guitar Gently Weeps" was unforgettable. We were walking on air for weeks afterwards.

Little did I know at the time that I'd be back in the same building thirty years later, in 2001, hosting the Concert for New York City. I'm so proud to have been a part of that night.

There were many questions in my head leading up to that show. How can you be funny for the families of firemen, policemen, and everybody else who had just lost loved ones, when everyone was walking around New York still stunned and in mourning? It was only a month after September 11. What could we do to alleviate their burden? Would they want to laugh, and if so, what kind of humor would be acceptable? It was the most challenging moment of my career.

I walked out onstage without an introduction and saw all these widows, widowers, and fatherless children holding up pictures of their lost fathers, mothers, sisters, brothers, cousins, and uncles. When I'm onstage I always try to look at the audience, but it was difficult that night. I was seeing all those desperate, sad faces saying, "Please, get this sadness off my shoulders for a little while." There were so many people holding up cards and 8 x 10 photos, with signs that read, "Have you seen my brother? Have you seen my father?"

It was daunting but it was also my greatest moment in the Garden. I was a player that night. I was a Band-Aid for a couple of hours, and the fact that my humor was welcomed, and seemed to provide some small relief, was very gratifying.

All of us came together for this great cause and, at the end of the show, it was surreal to be singing with Paul McCartney, Elton John, Eric Clapton, Jon Bon Jovi, Sheryl Crow, and The Who. I remember standing next to Jim Carrey; we were both crying. "Are we really here? Are we really a part of this? Are we really singing 'Let It Be' with Paul McCartney?!"

As I look back, I think both of these concerts could only have happened at the Garden. Madison Square Garden sits in the middle of Manhattan, in the heart of our city — and in the hearts of millions of New Yorkers.

August 1, 1971 – George Harrison at the Concert
for Bangladesh, the first major benefit concert.

Loraine & Peter Boyle

Lennon's Last Stand

The Thanksgiving leftovers were packed away in our fridge, and we were in a limo with our friend Yoko Ono on our way to Madison Square Garden. It was November 28, 1974, and there were rumors that John Lennon would perform there with Elton John that night. Yoko, who was separated from John at the time but still in touch with him, invited us to accompany her. For us it was slightly awkward, because we were also good friends with John and May Pang, his then-girlfriend. But nothing about the Lennons was ever conventional.

Our seats were primo — eleventh row on the floor. Other celebrities were in attendance, but all eyes were on the stage. Elton performed brilliantly and then, as if the heavens had opened up, with an intense strobe, John Lennon came onstage. This was the first time he had performed there since 1972 for the "One to One Concert" and, as it turned out, the last time he'd ever perform at Madison Square Garden. The audience exploded: May Pang , who was standing next to Elton's piano recalls, "I never felt anything like that in my life."

"Elton performed brilliantly and then, as if the heavens had opened up, with an intense strobe, John Lennon came onstage."

We felt the Garden shaking with the fans' excitement, as Elton and Lennon launched into Lennon's "Whatever Gets You Through The Night." Elton had played keyboards and sung backup on the song when John recorded it back in the early summer of 1974. Elton thought that the song was such a strong single that he proposed a deal: if it hit number one on the charts, John would appear at the Garden to perform the song with him. To Lennon's surprise, both the song and the album it came from, *Walls and Bridges*, did top the charts at number one, a first for John as a solo artist.

The audience couldn't get enough of the two of them, and the love and excitement of the crowd spurred them on. According to May, John had been nervous all day and the performance finally brought relief. Both superstars had practiced the number at the Record Plant the Sunday before and were ready to rock and roll together on two more numbers. To the crowd's delight they performed "Lucy In the Sky With Diamonds." John had traveled to the Caribou Ranch in Colorado to record that one with Elton. When that number brought down the house once again, Lennon told the jubilant crowd, "We tried to think of a number that we could finish off with so I can get outta here and be sick. And we thought we'd do a number of an old estranged fiancé of mine called Paul. This is one I never sang. It's an old Beatles number, and we just about know it." And then they launched into "I Saw Her Standing There."

It was a night we could never forget. The floor shook, as people stomped and cheered and hollered in excitement, while John Lennon performed once again in New York. Everyone sensed that this was a moment in history, and that after his carousing in Los Angeles, he had come home to play for his adopted hometown, in Madison Square Garden.

OPPOSITE
November 28, 1974 – John Lennon joined Elton John
on stage for three songs, in what would turn out
to be Lennon's last public performance.

ABOVE
August 16, 1984 – Luciano Pavarotti's magnetic
warmth and adoring audience called for six encores.

ABOVE
June 23, 1975 – The Rolling Stones stopped at the Garden
for five nights on their 1975 Tour of the Americas. Their
elaborate lotus-shaped stage included a twenty-five ton
flower with hydraulically controlled petals.

Phil Jackson **From All Sides**

I've seen this arena from many sides, as a player for the Knicks, as an opposing coach, as a fan attending concerts, and as a spectator at other sporting events.

As a Knick, I really felt like part of the Garden family. I got to partake in so many events, especially concerts. I saw Jackson Browne perform at the Felt Forum. I sat onstage at a Bob Dylan concert, watching my team-mate, Bill Bradley, snapping photos in the aisles. I sat onstage for the Rolling Stones. I didn't go to the Concert for Bangladesh, Bradley did. I don't know why I didn't go, and I still feel I should have been there. When you're a six-foot-nine professional basketball player with a beard, you can usually maneuver yourself onstage at a concert.

There is one night in the early 1970s that really epitomizes my relationship with the Garden. I started the evening playing for the Knicks against the Baltimore Bullets before a sellout crowd. Afterward, I wandered downstairs to the Felt Forum, the intimate 5,000-seat venue below the main arena, for a Grateful Dead concert. For a child of the sixties, playing for the Knicks and attending a Grateful Dead concert in one evening brought me close to nirvana. It was a double-header that could only happen at the Garden — I played in a Knicks game in front of more than 18,000 people, then went downstairs for a Dead concert with a whole different crowd of 5,000 more.

"We were out to change the world, and the music symbolized our rebellion. I think my whole generation started going to concerts back then. . ."

I also loved attending heavyweight fights at the Garden. In 1971, I went to the first Ali-Frazier fight, one of the liveliest nights you'd ever want to see. To me, because of his stand against the war, Ali was a true hero, far surpassing his exploits in the ring. I remember there was tension in the air that night, perhaps because of all the political symbolism of the match. But there was unequaled excitement as well. There's nothing like the atmosphere of a heavyweight fight, and that night was thrilling.

Taking my Garden music experience full circle, I went to a Phish concert with my kids on New Year's Eve 1998. That was the last Garden concert I've attended. I think of Phish as this generation's Grateful Dead, maybe because their faithful followers go with them from concert to concert, like the Dead fans used to do.

Living through that era made me realize that attending concerts was about more than the music. There was a cultural revolution going on—in civil rights, in politics, and in fashion.

I often think back to my first visit to New York, on Memorial Day weekend in 1967, right after the Knicks had drafted me. Arriving in New York from North Dakota, I ran smack into a huge demonstration in Manhattan — 500,000 people marching in support of the Vietnam War. Firemen, policemen, and sanitation workers all marched, proving that New York was not just a city of liberals, it was a city up for grabs.

OPPOSITE
October 1994 – The Grateful Dead played the Garden for the fifty-second and last time, setting a record — since broken by Elton John — for the most perform-ances at the Garden by any group or performer.

"[Madison Square Garden is]
the greatest rock room."

—TOM PETTY

I was a part of that generation that protested the war. With my long hair and beard, I felt I was lucky to be a New York Knick, playing basketball in a city that tolerated differences. You know, we were one of the few teams that allowed beards and mustaches and long hair — other teams wouldn't tolerate it. So being in a relatively liberal space allowed me the opportunity to express myself as an individual.

And in attending those concerts at the Garden, I felt a unity and a love for the rest of the audience. We were out to change the world, and the music symbolized our rebellion. I think my whole generation started going to concerts back then, and we've never stopped.

ABOVE
November 28, 2001 – Elton John played at the Garden
for the fifty-third time, setting a new Garden record.

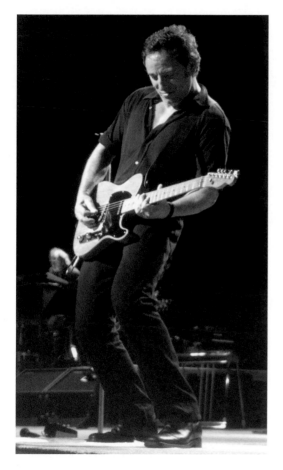

LEFT
July, 2000 – Bruce Springsteen and the E Street Band's world tour culminated in ten sold-out shows at the Garden, which were recorded for a live CD and an HBO special.

TOP
September 29, 2000 – Barbra Streisand played two nights at the Garden for her farewell concert.

BOTTOM RIGHT
December 31, 1999 – Billy Joel rang in the new millenium with a special New Year's Eve concert.

125 Greatest Moments at Madison Square Garden

Boxing

July 17, 1882
John L. Sullivan vs. Joe Collins.

March 25, 1916
Jess Willard vs. Frank Moran.

December 14, 1920
Jack Dempsey vs. Bill Brennan.

May 23, 1922
Gene Tunney vs. Harry Greb.

January 16, 1942
Sugar Ray Robinson vs. Fritzie Zivic.

February 23, 1945
Sugar Ray Robinson vs. Jake LaMotta.

December 5, 1947
Joe Louis vs. Jersey Joe Wolcott.

February 11, 1949
Sandy Saddler vs. Willie Pep.

October 26, 1951
Joe Louis vs. Rocky Marciano.

March 13, 1963
Cassius Clay (Muhammad Ali)
vs. Doug Jones.

April 25, 1966
Emile Griffith vs. Dick Tiger.

March 4, 1968
Joe Frazier vs. Buster Mathis.

March 8, 1971
Muhammad Ali vs. Joe Frazier —
the "Fight of the Century."

June 26, 1972
Roberto Duran vs. Ken Buchanan.

January 28, 1974
Muhammad Ali vs. Joe Frazier II.

June 16, 1983
Roberto Duran vs. Davey Moore.

March 13, 1999
Evander Holyfield vs. Lennox Lewis.

September 29, 2001
Bernard Hopkins vs. Felix Trinidad.

January 26, 2002
"Sugar" Shane Mosley vs. Vernon Forrest.

Knicks

November 11, 1946
The Knicks make their home debut.

October 28, 1950
Nat "Sweetwater" Clifton breaks the
Knicks color barrier and plays his first
game at the Garden.

January 21, 1954
The Garden hosts the NBA All-Star Game
for the first time.

November 16, 1962
Wilt Chamberlain scores 73, a Garden
record.

May 4, 1970
The Knicks, down by 20, rally to defeat
the Lakers in Game Five of the Finals.

May 8, 1970
Willis Reed returns from an injury and the
Knicks win their first NBA championship.

November 18, 1972
The Knicks rally to defeat the Bucks in
their greatest regular-season comeback.

April 22, 1973
The Knicks score a double-overtime
playoff win over the Celtics.

December 25, 1984
Bernard King scores a franchise-record
60 points against the Nets.

May 25, 1993
John Starks' dunk over the Bulls in Game
Two, Eastern Conference Finals.

June 1, 1994
The Pacer's Reggie Miller scores 25 points
in the fourth quarter of Game Five of the
Conference Semifinals.

June 5, 1994
Knicks win the Eastern Conference.

March 28, 1995
Michael Jordan returns to the NBA after
his first retirement and scores 55 points.

June 5, 1999
Larry Johnson's four-point play against
the Pacers in Game Three of the Eastern
Conference Finals.

June 11, 1999
Knicks win the Eastern Conference.

February 28, 2003
Patrick Ewing Night; his number is retired.

Liberty

June 29, 1997
First game ever for the New York Liberty
at the Garden.

July 14, 1999
First WNBA All-Star Game takes place
before a sell-out crowd.

August 21, 2000
Liberty win the Eastern Conference.

College Basketball

December 29, 1934
First double-header at MSG, promoted by Ned Irish and featuring St. John's vs. Westminster and Notre Dame vs. NYU.

December 30, 1936
In a "dream match," Stanford defeats LIU (undefeated in 43 straight) 45-31, as Hank Luisetti's one-handed shooting style changes the game of basketball.

March 14, 1946
A sold-out crowd watches as Ernie Calverley of Rhode Island makes a 55' basket at the buzzer to tie Bowling Green in the NIT Quarterfinals. Rhode Island wins in overtime.

March 28, 1950
CCNY defeats Bradley for the NCAA title.

January 9, 1958
Oscar Robertson's 56 points sets a Garden collegiate scoring record.

December 30, 1964
Bradley scores 41 in a Holiday Festival semifinal loss to Michigan.

January 2, 1965
St. John's defeats Michigan to win the Holiday Festival.

March 20, 1965
St. John's wins the NIT title in Joe Lapchick's final game as coach.

February 22, 1975
Immaculata College defeats Queens College 65-61 in the first women's college game at the Garden.

March 6, 1977
Carol Blazejowski scores 52 points, a collegiate scoring record for Garden IV.

March 12, 1983
St. John's wins the first Big East Tournament.

February 2, 1991
St. John's coach Lou Carnesecca records his 500th victory.

Miscellaneous

May 31, 1879
Madison Square Garden is inaugurated with a gala concert.

June 16, 1890
Opening day of the Stanford White-designed Garden II.

June 25, 1906
Stanford White is murdered on the Garden's rooftop.

May 5, 1925
The final event at Garden II is a boxing match between lightweights Sid Terris and Johnny Dundee.

November 25, 1925
Garden III opens with a six-day bike race.

January 8, 1929
Tex Rickard lays "in-state" at the Garden and thousands of admirers pay their respects.

October 17, 1957
Mike Todd throws a party for his movie *Around the World in 80 Days* and wife Elizabeth Taylor hosts.

May 19, 1962
Marilyn Monroe sings "Happy Birthday" to President John F. Kennedy.

February 11, 1968
Bob Hope and Bing Crosby host a USO show to open Garden IV.

October 15, 1969
MSG Network is born with a telecast of a Rangers-North Stars game.

October 3, 1979
Pope John Paul II visits the Garden.

May 18, 1982
Reverend Sun Myung Moon of the Unification Church performs a mass wedding.

April 23, 1989
Gunther Gebel-Williams' performs for the final time at the Garden.

November 23, 1994
A Christmas Carol opens in the Theater, and runs during the holiday season for ten years.

February 26, 1997
The Garden hosts the Grammy Awards, the first time they are held in an arena.

October 27, 1998
MSG Network's first HDTV telecast, a Rangers–Sabres game.

December 2, 1999
Sports Illustrated's "Athlete of the Century" event.

February 26, 2002
MSG Network is re-launched as a 24-hour cable network.

Rangers

November 16, 1926
Rangers first game ever.

March 27, 1938
Rangers vs. Americans — longest Rangers game in Garden history ends during the fourth overtime.

December 3, 1947
Lester Patrick Night.

January 25, 1967
Harry Howell Night.

February 11, 1968
Last Rangers game at Garden III. Every living Hall of Fame Rangers player attends.

April 5, 1970
Rangers beat the Red Wings 9-5 in the final regular-season game, which the Rangers needed to win with a high goal total to qualify for the playoffs over the Canadiens.

April 29, 1971
Pete Stemkowski scores the winning goal in triple-overtime against the Blackhawks in the Cup Semifinals.

January 30, 1973
The Garden hosts the NHL All-Star Game for the first time.

November 2, 1975
Eddie Giacomin returns to the Garden after being traded to the Red Wings.

May 8, 1979
The Rangers defeat the rival Islanders and advance to the Stanley Cup Finals.

October 7, 1991
Mark Messier plays his first game as a Ranger at the Garden.

January 22, 1994
The Garden hosts its second NHL All-Star Game and Mike Richter is named MVP.

May 27, 1994
Stephane Matteau's double-overtime goal in Game Seven clinches the Eastern Division title for the Rangers.

June 14, 1994
The Rangers win the Stanley Cup.

April 18, 1999
Wayne Gretzky's final NHL game.

February 4, 2004
Mike Richter Night; his number is retired.

Politics

October 26, 1900
Teddy Roosevelt delivers a rousing speech to an overflow crowd at the Garden as a Republican candidate for Vice President.

June 26, 1924
Franklin Delano Roosevelt nominates Al Smith with the "Happy Warrior" speech at the 1924 Democratic National Convention.

July 15, 1976
The Democrats nominate Jimmy Carter for President.

July 16, 1992
Bill Clinton accepts the Democratic Party nomination for President.

Sports

May 11, 1880
First Westminster Kennel Club Dog Show is held.

October 22, 1883
The first National Horse Show is held at the Garden.

January 11, 1896
Frankie Nelson wins the first Women's Bicycle Marathon, a six-day race.

February 5, 1930
Sonja Henie wins the World Championship of Skating.

February 21, 1934
Tennis great Bill Tilden defeats Henri Cochet in five sets in what some call the greatest match of Tilden's career.

February 4, 1939
Glenn Cunningham wins his sixth Wanamaker Mile, a record that stood until Eamonn Coghlan won his seventh in 1987.

February 7, 1942
Cornelius Warmerdam becomes the first indoor 15' pole vaulter with a vault of 15' 3/8" in the Millrose Games.

December 26, 1947
Over 15,000 fans brave a blizzard that buries the city with 26" of snow to watch tennis greats Jack Kramer and Bobby Riggs.

January 31, 1959
Seventeen-year-old John Thomas clears 7' in the high jump, the first time the 7' mark is reached indoors.

February 2, 1961
Wilma Rudolph ties her own women's indoor record in the 60-yard dash.

February 9, 1968
Jim Ryun wins "The Last Garden Mile" in the final track meet at Garden III.

March 28, 1976
Nadia Comaneci records the first perfect 10 in gymnastics at the American Cup.

February 8, 1980
Mary Decker establishes a world indoor record for 1500 meters with a time of 4:00.8 at the Millrose Games.

February 25, 1983
Carl Lewis wins both the 60 meter dash (6:04) and the long jump (27' 4") at the National Indoor Championships.

March 31, 1985
The first WrestleMania®.

January 30, 1987
Eamonn Coghlan wins a record seventh Wanamaker Mile at the Millrose Games.

February 3, 1989
Jackie Joyner-Kersee sets a world indoor record (7.37) in the 55-meter hurdles at the Millrose Games.

Concerts

December 25, 1967
Judy Garland performs at the newly opened Felt Forum.

May 18, 1969
Jimi Hendrix plays the Garden.

November 27, 1969
The Rolling Stones make their Garden debut.

December 19, 1969
Janis Joplin and the Kozmic Blues Band play the Garden.

August 1, 1971
George Harrison presents the Concert for Bangladesh.

June 9, 1972
Elvis Presley plays the Garden.

June 5, 1974
Sly and the Family Stone concert and on-stage wedding.

October 12, 1974
Frank Sinatra's "The Main Event."

November 28, 1974
John Lennon performs with Elton John.

September 22, 1979
No Nukes concert.

August 16, 1984
Luciano Pavarotti performs, the first classical music performance at Garden IV.

March 3, 1988
Michael Jackson plays the Garden.

October 16, 1992
Concert tribute to Bob Dylan.

October 6, 1993
First of twenty consecutive nights in The Theater for Simon & Garfunkel.

October 14, 1993
Madonna's "The Girlie Show" tour.

October 19, 1994
The Grateful Dead play the Garden for the final time.

December 31, 1999
Billy Joel rings in the new millennium.

July 1, 2000
Bruce Springsteen concludes his world tour with ten sold out nights at the Garden.

September 29, 2000
Barbra Streisand ends her live concert performance career at the Garden.

October 20, 2001
The Concert for New York City.

Copyright © 2004 George Kalinsky and Madison Square Garden, L.P.

Introduction copyright © 2004 Pete Hamill.

Essay on page 146-49, "How Did He Do That?" copyright © 2004 William H. Cosby, Jr.

All photographs from the lens of George Kalinsky except AP Wide World Photos: 86, 101, 141; Bruce Bennett: 107, 114, 115, 118; Nathaniel S. Butler/Getty Images/NBAE: 70; Corbis Images: 28, 29, 31, 51, 85, 86, 94, 95, 126, 164; MSG Archives: 18, 24-25, 28; MSG Photos/Dave Saffran: 71, 78, 80, 81; MSG Photos/Rebecca Taylor: 80, 118, 150; Museum of the City of NY: 16; Kevin Mazur: 189; N. Y. Daily News: 29, 147, 149; NY Knicks Archive: 58, 59; NY Life Archives: 14, 17; NY Rangers Archive: 109, 110; World Wrestling Entertainment: 163 (© 2004 World Wrestling Entertainment, Inc.)

Published in 2004 by
Stewart, Tabori & Chang
115 West 18th Street
New York, NY 10011
www.abramsbooks.com

Canadian Distribution:
Canadian Manda Group
One Atlantic Avenue, Suite 105
Toronto, Ontario M6K 3E7
Canada

Library of Congress Cataloging-in-Publication Data
Madison Square Garden.
    Garden of dreams : Madison Square Garden 125 years / photographs by George Kalinsky; introduction by Pete Hamill. — 1st ed.
      p. cm.
    ISBN 1-58479-343-0 (hardcover)
1. Madison Square Garden (New York, N.Y.) — History. 2. Madison Square Garden (New York, N.Y.) — History — Pictorial works. 3. Arenas — New York (State) — New York — History. 4. Arenas — New York (State) — New York — History — Pictorial works. I. Title.
GV416.N48K35 2004
796.06'09747'1 — dc22
                    2004012623

Designed by Geoff Ledet

The text of this book was composed in Signa and Verdigris.

Printed in the United States of America

10 9 8 7 6 5 4 3 2

Stewart, Tabori & Chang is a subsidiary of